CONGRESSIONAL POLICIES, PRACTICES AND PROCEDURES

THE FEDERAL BUDGET

2013 AND BEYOND

CONGRESSIONAL POLICIES, PRACTICES AND PROCEDURES

Additional books in this series can be found on Nova's website under the Series tab.

Additional E-books in this series can be found on Nova's website under the E-book tab.

ECONOMIC ISSUES, PROBLEMS AND PERSPECTIVES

Additional books in this series can be found on Nova's website under the Series tab.

Additional E-books in this series can be found on Nova's website under the E-book tab.

CONGRESSIONAL POLICIES, PRACTICES AND PROCEDURES

THE FEDERAL BUDGET

2013 AND BEYOND

JACOB E. LAMBERT
AND
ISABELLA M. JOHNSON
EDITORS

nova publishers
New York

For permission to use material from this book please contact us:
Telephone 631-231-7269; Fax 631-231-8175
Web Site: http://www.novapublishers.com

Library of Congress Cataloging-in-Publication Data

ISBN: 978-1-62081-920-3

Published by Nova Science Publishers, Inc. † New York

CONTENTS

PREFACE

The federal budget is central to Congress's ability to exercise its "power of the purse." Federal budget decisions also express Congress's priorities and reinforce Congress's influence on federal policies. Making budgetary decisions for the federal government is a complex process and requires balancing competing goals. Recent economic turmoil has strained the federal budget as a result of declining revenues and increasing spending levels. As the economic recovery continues, the budget process will allow the President and Congress to negotiate priorities and refine spending plans. This book examines issues for the FY 2013 federal budget with a focus on the rising costs of entitlement programs, significant spending on overseas military operations, and low revenue levels. While the economy is growing again, unemployment remains elevated and government spending on "automatic stabilizers," such as unemployment insurance and income security programs, remains higher than historical averages.

Chapter 1 – The federal budget is central to Congress's ability to exercise its "power of the purse." Over the last several fiscal years the imbalance between spending and revenues has grown as a result of the economic downturn and policies enacted in response to financial turmoil. In FY2011, the US government spent \$3,598 billion (24.1% of GDP) and collected \$2,302 billion in revenue (15.4% of GDP), resulting in a budget deficit of \$1,296 billion (8.7% of GDP). The FY2012 deficit is currently estimated at \$1,079 billion (7.0% of GDP).

The Obama Administration released its FY2013 budget on February 13, 2012. In FY2013, the President's budget projects that the deficit will reach \$901 billion. Budget deficits are projected throughout the 10-year budget window. The President's budget proposes a variety of short-term tax and spending measures aimed at job creation, largely drawn from the American Jobs Act submitted to Congress in September 2011. These proposals amount to nearly $350 billion in additional spending and tax cuts, including immediate funding for roads, rails, and runways; aid to states and local governments for teachers and first responders; school modernization; and a full-year extension of the Social Security payroll tax reduction and unemployment benefits.

In August 2011, the Budget Control Act of 2011 (BCA) placed limits on spending via discretionary spending caps and included provisions for additional spending cuts in the amount of $1.2 trillion. In January 2013, the additional cuts are scheduled to take effect via an automatic process. In his FY2013 budget, President Obama proposes replacing the automatic cuts with prescribed spending cuts and tax increases. The largest of these proposals includes allowing the 2001/2003/2010 tax cuts for singles making over $200,000 and households making over $250,000 to expire; savings generated from changes to Medicare, Medicaid, agriculture, and other mandatory programs; and placing caps on spending on Overseas Contingency Operations (OCO).

The FY2013 budget also included other tax proposals including changes in the estate tax parameters, limits to the value of itemized deductions for married taxpayers with incomes over $250,000 and single taxpayers with incomes over $200,000, and eliminating various tax expenditures. The Administration also released a framework for corporate tax reform, which included a reduction in the corporate tax rate combined with an elimination of certain corporate tax expenditures. The Administration is committed to reform that would not add to the deficit.

On March 21, 2012, the House Budget Committee reported the budget resolution (H.Con.Res. 112, 112th Congress) by a vote of 19-18. The resolution provided for revenue levels of $2,734 billion and outlays of $3,530 billion in FY2013 for a deficit of $797 billion, or approximately 5.0% of GDP. By FY2022, the deficit is projected to fall to $287 billion or 1.2% of GDP. Like the President's budget proposal, the House budget resolution specifies a replacement of the BCA's automatic cuts. The budget resolution replaces the majority of the cuts in FY2013 with $261 billion in deficit reduction over 10 years to be achieved via reconciliation.

CBO, GAO, and the Administration agree that the current mix of federal fiscal policies is unsustainable in the long term. The nation's aging population, combined with rising health care costs per beneficiary, seems likely to keep federal health costs rising faster than per capita GDP.

Chapter 2 – In 2009, the federal budget deficit (the difference between outlays and revenues) exceeded $1 trillion for the first time, and it has remained above $1 trillion since. Those years also marked the largest the deficit has been as a share of gross domestic product (GDP) in the period since World War II. The budget is not projected to be on a sustainable path under current policy, in the sense that it leads the publicly held debt to continuously grow more quickly than GDP. The timing of deficit reduction remains a difficult issue because of continued weakness in the economy.

If deficits are reduced too quickly, the economy might tip back into recession. If unsustainable deficits persist for too long in the economic recovery, it could crowd out private investment and, in the worst case scenario, investors could refuse to continue to finance deficits that they believed were unsustainable.

As one example of the policy changes that would return the budget to a sustainable path, the Congressional Research Service (CRS) estimates that stabilizing debt as a share of GDP at its 2011 level would require budget deficits averaging 2.8% of GDP over the next 10 years. In dollar terms, the deficit could equal $200 billion in 2013, rising to more than $600 billion from 2015 on.

Under the Congressional Budget Office's (CBO's) current law baseline, the deficit is already on a sustainable path. Under CBO's Alternative Fiscal Scenario, which modifies the current law baseline by assuming that expiring tax provisions and the "doc fix" to Medicare are extended and that the future automatic spending cuts under the Budget Control Act (BCA) do not come into effect, the deficit would decline from more than 9% of GDP in 2011 to 5% of GDP in 2015, then rise to 6% of GDP by 2022. To reduce the deficit to sustainable levels under this scenario would require some combination of spending cuts and tax increases equivalent to roughly $800 billion in 2013, falling to $275 billion in 2015, then rising to $900 billion by 2022.

The recent growth in deficits is the result of spending reaching its highest level as a share of GDP since 1945 and revenues reaching their lowest level as a share of GDP since 1950. Revenues were low because of the recession and because of the temporary extension of expiring tax provisions, such as the "alternative minimum tax (AMT) patch" and "Bush tax cuts."

If these tax cuts are extended again, revenues are estimated to be reduced by about 2.5% of GDP from 2014 on and will remain around their historical average from 2015 on.

Thus far, policy changes to reduce the deficit have targeted mainly discretionary spending. The BCA would reduce discretionary spending by

$1.5 trillion and mandatory spending by less than $0.2 trillion over 10 years if automatic cuts are allowed to begin in 2013. Including interest savings, the BCA would reduce the deficit by about 1% of GDP from 2014 on.

Even if these cuts proceed as scheduled, overall spending is projected to rise and remain above its historical average over the next 10 years because of the growth in mandatory spending. Defense, Social Security, and Medicare account for more than half of total spending. Outside of those three programs and net interest, all other spending is about three-quarters the size of the budget deficit in 2012.

Growth in entitlement spending on the elderly drives long-term projections of large budget deficits—by mid-century, outlays on Social Security and health programs would exceed total revenues. Most proposals to reform entitlement programs for the elderly would generate significant budgetary savings in the long run, but little budgetary savings in the short run, partly because most proposals exempt current retirees from reform and partly because the savings from these changes would compound over time.

The US fiscal outlook is not a purely long-term issue, however—deficits are already at unsustainably high levels today.

Chapter 3 – The Budget Control Act of 2011 (BCA) was signed into law by President Obama on August 2, 2011 (P.L. 112-25). In addition to increasing the debt limit, the BCA contained a variety of measures intended to reduce the deficit by at least $2.1 trillion over the FY2012-FY2021 period.

These included $917 billion in savings from statutory caps on discretionary spending and the establishment of a Joint Select Committee on Deficit Reduction.

The BCA discretionary spending caps are projected to result in $917 billion in deficit reduction over the FY2012-FY2021 period. Some types of spending are not subject to the caps, including for spending on Overseas Contingency Operations and emergencies. The precise programmatic impact of these reductions in discretionary spending will be determined in the annual appropriations process. Under the Congressional Budget Office's (CBO's) August 2011 baseline, which incorporates the effects of the BCA, the discretionary spending caps result in a decline in spending in nominal dollar terms in FY2012 and FY2013. Discretionary spending under the caps is projected to decline from 9.0% of GDP in FY2011 to 6.2% of gross domestic product (GDP) in FY2021. Since FY1962, the first year for which data are available, discretionary spending as a percentage of GDP has only been that low in one other year (FY1999).

Beyond the BCA's deficit reduction achieved via the discretionary spending caps, the Joint Committee was created to find additional deficit reduction.

On November 21, 2011, the co-chairs of the Joint Committee announced that they were unable to reach an agreement before the committee's deadline. As a result, a $1.2 trillion automatic spending reduction process has been triggered to begin in January 2013 unless Congress and the President act to eliminate or change the process before then.

The automatic reduction would be divided evenly between defense and non-defense spending. Many large mandatory programs are exempt from this process. The automatic reduction in spending for non-exempt accounts in FY2013 is projected to be 10% for defense, 2% for Medicare, and 7.8% for other mandatory and non-defense discretionary, resulting in further deficit reduction of $1.1 trillion between FY2013 and FY2021. Overall, 85% of the automatic spending cuts in FY2014 are projected to fall on discretionary programs.

Cuts to discretionary spending through the automatic reduction would be in addition to those cuts resulting from the discretionary spending caps. After taking those two provisions into account, total discretionary spending would not regain its 2011 level until 2021 in nominal terms.

While the BCA is projected to reduce the deficit, it does not eliminate budget deficits or growth in the federal debt over the 10-year budget window. Using a current law baseline (where a series of tax cuts are assumed to expire and controls on Medicare payments to doctors are allowed to take effect), budget deficits are estimated to total $3.6 trillion and the federal debt is projected to increase by $4.4 trillion over the next 10 years. Under a current policy baseline (where a series of tax cuts are extended and controls on Medicare payments to doctors are not allowed to take effect), deficits over the next 10 years total $8.6 trillion and the debt would continue to rise faster than GDP. Since the debt cannot perpetually rise faster than GDP, additional spending cuts or revenue increases would eventually be needed.

Since deficit reduction under the BCA is relatively small in FY2012, the short-term effects on the economy should be limited. In the long run, economic theory suggests that large deficits would have negative effects on interest rates, investment spending, trade deficits, and GDP.

Chapter 4 – In conjunction with its analysis of the President's budget, which will be issued in a few days, the Congressional Budget Office (CBO) has updated the baseline budget projections that it released in January. CBO has not revised its assessment of the economic outlook since January;

however, the new baseline projections incorporate the budgetary effects of recently enacted legislation and updated technical assumptions based on new information (such as data about spending and revenues so far this year and program details released in conjunction with the President's budget).

This report summarizes CBO's updated baseline budget projections and describes how they differ from the projections that the agency published two months earlier.

CBO's current estimate of the budget deficit for fiscal year 2012—$1.2 trillion—is $93 billion larger than the deficit projected in January. Conversely, CBO's baseline projection of the cumulative deficit for the 10-year period from 2013 to 2022 is $186 billion smaller than the amount projected in January—a decrease equal to about 0.1 percent of gross domestic product (GDP) over that period. The fundamental story about the federal budget has not changed: Although the deficit is starting to shrink, it remains very large by historical standards.

How much and how quickly it declines will depend in part on how well the economy performs over the next few years. Probably more critical, though, will be the fiscal policy choices made by lawmakers as they face the substantial changes to tax and spending policies that are slated to take effect within the next year under current law.

Chapter 5 – This report by the Congressional Budget Office (CBO) presents an analysis of the proposals contained in the President's budget request for fiscal year 2013.

The analysis is based on CBO's economic projections and estimating techniques (rather than the Administration's) and incorporates estimates by the staff of the Joint Committee on Taxation for the President's tax proposals.

In conjunction with analyzing the President's budget, CBO has updated its baseline budget projections, which were previously issued in January 2012. Unlike its estimates of the President's budget, CBO's baseline projections largely reflect the assumption that current tax and spending laws will remain unchanged, so as to provide a benchmark against which potential legislation can be measured. Under that assumption, CBO estimates that the deficit would total $1.2 trillion in 2012 and that cumulative deficits over the 2013–2022 period would amount to $2.9 trillion.

The President's budget request specifies spending and revenue policies for the 2013–2022 period and also includes initiatives that would have budgetary effects in fiscal year 2012.

Chapter 6 – Since 1992, GAO has published long-term fiscal simulations showing federal deficits and debt under different sets of policy assumptions.

GAO developed its long-term model in response to a bipartisan request from members of Congress concerned about the long-term effects of fiscal policy. GAO's simulations provide context for consideration of policy options. They are not intended to suggest particular policy choices or to predict the economic impact of any set of choices but to help facilitate a dialogue on this important issue.

GAO regularly updates its simulations as new data become available from the Congressional Budget Office (CBO) and the Social Security and Medicare Trustees (Trustees). This update incorporates CBO's January 2012 budget and economic projections.

In: The Federal Budget: 2013 and Beyond ISBN: 978-1-62081-920-3
Editors: J. Lambert and I. Johnson

Chapter 1

THE FEDERAL BUDGET: ISSUES FOR FY2013 AND BEYOND*

Mindy R. Levit

SUMMARY

The federal budget is central to Congress's ability to exercise its "power of the purse." Over the last several fiscal years the imbalance between spending and revenues has grown as a result of the economic downturn and policies enacted in response to financial turmoil. In FY2011, the US government spent $3,598 billion (24.1% of GDP) and collected $2,302 billion in revenue (15.4% of GDP), resulting in a budget deficit of $1,296 billion (8.7% of GDP). The FY2012 deficit is currently estimated at $1,079 billion (7.0% of GDP).

The Obama Administration released its FY2013 budget on February 13, 2012. In FY2013, the President's budget projects that the deficit will reach $901 billion. Budget deficits are projected throughout the 10-year budget window. The President's budget proposes a variety of short-term tax and spending measures aimed at job creation, largely drawn from the American Jobs Act submitted to Congress in September 2011. These proposals amount to nearly $350 billion in additional spending and tax cuts, including immediate funding for roads, rails, and runways; aid to states and local governments for teachers and first responders; school

* This is an edited, reformatted and augmented version of a Congressional Research Service publication, CRS Report for Congress R42362, from www.crs.gov, prepared for Members and Committees of Congress, dated March 27, 2012.

modernization; and a full-year extension of the Social Security payroll tax reduction and unemployment benefits.

In August 2011, the Budget Control Act of 2011 (BCA) placed limits on spending via discretionary spending caps and included provisions for additional spending cuts in the amount of $1.2 trillion. In January 2013, the additional cuts are scheduled to take effect via an automatic process. In his FY2013 budget, President Obama proposes replacing the automatic cuts with prescribed spending cuts and tax increases. The largest of these proposals includes allowing the 2001/2003/2010 tax cuts for singles making over $200,000 and households making over $250,000 to expire; savings generated from changes to Medicare, Medicaid, agriculture, and other mandatory programs; and placing caps on spending on Overseas Contingency Operations (OCO).

The FY2013 budget also included other tax proposals including changes in the estate tax parameters, limits to the value of itemized deductions for married taxpayers with incomes over $250,000 and single taxpayers with incomes over $200,000, and eliminating various tax expenditures. The Administration also released a framework for corporate tax reform, which included a reduction in the corporate tax rate combined with an elimination of certain corporate tax expenditures. The Administration is committed to reform that would not add to the deficit.

On March 21, 2012, the House Budget Committee reported the budget resolution (H.Con.Res. 112, 112th Congress) by a vote of 19-18. The resolution provided for revenue levels of $2,734 billion and outlays of $3,530 billion in FY2013 for a deficit of $797 billion, or approximately 5.0% of GDP. By FY2022, the deficit is projected to fall to $287 billion or 1.2% of GDP. Like the President's budget proposal, the House budget resolution specifies a replacement of the BCA's automatic cuts. The budget resolution replaces the majority of the cuts in FY2013 with $261 billion in deficit reduction over 10 years to be achieved via reconciliation.

CBO, GAO, and the Administration agree that the current mix of federal fiscal policies is unsustainable in the long term. The nation's aging population, combined with rising health care costs per beneficiary, seems likely to keep federal health costs rising faster than per capita GDP.

INTRODUCTION

The federal budget is central to Congress's ability to exercise its "power of the purse." Federal budget decisions also express Congress's priorities and reinforce Congress's influence on federal policies. Making budgetary decisions for the federal government is a complex process and requires balancing competing goals. Recent economic turmoil has strained the federal budget as a result of declining revenues and increasing spending levels. As the economic recovery continues, the budget process will allow the President and Congress to negotiate priorities and refine spending plans.[1]

The federal government faces very large budget deficits, rising costs of entitlement programs, significant spending on overseas military operations, and low revenue levels. The enactment of financial intervention and fiscal stimulus legislation in FY2008 and FY2009 may have helped to bolster the economy, though they increased the budget deficit.[2] While the economy is growing again, unemployment remains elevated and government spending on "automatic stabilizers," such as unemployment insurance and income security programs, remains higher than historical averages.[3] This suggests that the recession's effects on the budget will likely remain for several more fiscal years.

In addition to the current challenges, concerns remain about the federal government's long-term fiscal situation. Work on improving the budget outlook resulted in the enactment of the Budget Control Act of 2011 (BCA; P.L. 112-25), which contained provisions to reduce the budget deficit by about $2 trillion over the next decade.[4] However, the rising costs of federal health care programs and the effects of the baby boom generation's retirement, which present serious challenges to future fiscal stability, have yet to be addressed. Operating these programs in their current form may pass on substantial economic burdens to future generations. To avoid this would require additional government action and public sacrifice at levels greater than those needed to counteract the recent economic downturn.

OVERVIEW

Budget Cycle

A single year's budget cycle takes roughly three calendar years from initial formation by the Office of Management and Budget (OMB) until final audit.[5] The executive agencies begin the budget process by compiling detailed budget requests in the calendar year before the President's budget submission. Many agencies start working on their budgets during the spring and summer—about a year and a half before the fiscal year begins. OMB oversees the development of these agency requests. The President is required to submit a budget to Congress, which is based on OMB's work, by the first Monday in February or about 8 months before the fiscal year begins.[6]

Congress typically begins formal consideration of the budget resolution once the President submits his budget request. The budget resolution sets out a plan, agreed to by the House and Senate, that establishes the framework for subsequent budget legislation. Because the budget resolution is a concurrent resolution, it is not sent to the President for approval.[7]

House and Senate Appropriations Committees and their subcommittees typically begin reporting discretionary spending bills after the budget resolution is agreed upon. Appropriations Committees review agency funding requests and propose levels of budget authority (BA). Appropriations acts passed by Congress set the amount of BA available for specific programs and activities. Authorizing committees, which control mandatory spending, and committees with jurisdiction over revenues also play important roles in budget decision making.[8]

During the fiscal year, which begins on October 1, Congress and OMB oversee the execution of the budget. Once the fiscal year ends on the following September 30, the Treasury Department and the Government Accountability Office (GAO) begin year-end audits.

Budget Baseline Projections

Budget baseline projections are used to measure how future legislation would affect the budget picture. They are not meant to be predictions of the future budget outlook. Due to the nature of projections, slight changes in assumptions can lead to large effects in outyear totals. Therefore, it is important to understand what projections include and the assumptions on which they are based. Baseline projections are included in both the President's budget and the Congressional budget resolution.

The Congressional Budget Office (CBO) computes current law baseline projections using assumptions set out in budget enforcement legislation.[9] Forecasts based on these assumptions typically yield higher revenue estimates and may understate discretionary spending levels. More specifically, CBO baseline projections incorporate certain assumptions: that the 2001/2003/2010 tax cuts fully expire after 2012 (as current law specifies), that one-year "patches" to the alternative minimum tax (AMT) will lapse even though past Congresses have extended AMT patches year after year, that sharp reductions in Medicare's payment rates for physician services will take effect as scheduled, and that extensions of unemployment compensation and the payroll tax cut will expire per current law. Baseline discretionary spending levels are based on the caps currently in law, with adjustments for war funding and disaster spending. In addition to these current law assumptions, macroeconomic assumptions, specifically of GDP growth, inflation, and interest rates, will also affect the baseline estimates and projections, especially given the current economic climate. Baseline projections show substantial growth in receipts after 2012, when most of the tax cuts from 2001/2003/2010 expire. This results in budget deficits that would reduce the level of debt as a percentage of GDP, particularly after FY2013. In other words, these budget deficits would be fiscally sustainable. Under the baseline assumptions, budget deficits are projected to average 1.5% of GDP over the FY2013 to FY2022 period.

CBO also provided projections based on alternative policy assumptions, which illustrate the levels of spending and revenue if current laws continue, rather than expire as scheduled. If the 2001/2003/2010 tax cuts are extended, the AMT is indexed for inflation, Medicare payment rates for physician services remain the same, and the provisions of the Budget Control Act's automatic spending reduction process do not take effect, CBO projects budget deficits to average 5.4% of GDP over the FY2013 to FY2022 period. Cumulative budget deficits under the alternative fiscal scenario are projected to be $7.9 trillion higher over the next decade (totaling $11.0 trillion) than under the baseline scenario.

Beyond the 10-year forecast window, federal deficits are expected to grow rapidly unless major policy changes are made. This is a result of rapidly growing outlays largely attributable to health care costs and baby boomer retirements.

Spending and Revenue Trends

Over the last four decades, on average, federal spending accounted for approximately 21% of the economy (as measured by gross domestic product—GDP), while federal revenues averaged roughly 18% of GDP. Since FY2001, spending has exceeded revenues, resulting in budget deficits. Over the last several fiscal years the imbalance between spending and revenues has grown as a result of the economic downturn and policies enacted in response to financial turmoil. In FY2011, the most recently completed fiscal year, the US government spent $3.6 trillion and collected $2.3 trillion in revenue. Relative to FY2008, FY2011 outlays increased by $616 billion while revenues decreased by $222 billion (in nominal terms). The trends in revenues and outlays between FY1970 and FY2011 are shown in *Figure 1*.

(as a percentage of GDP)

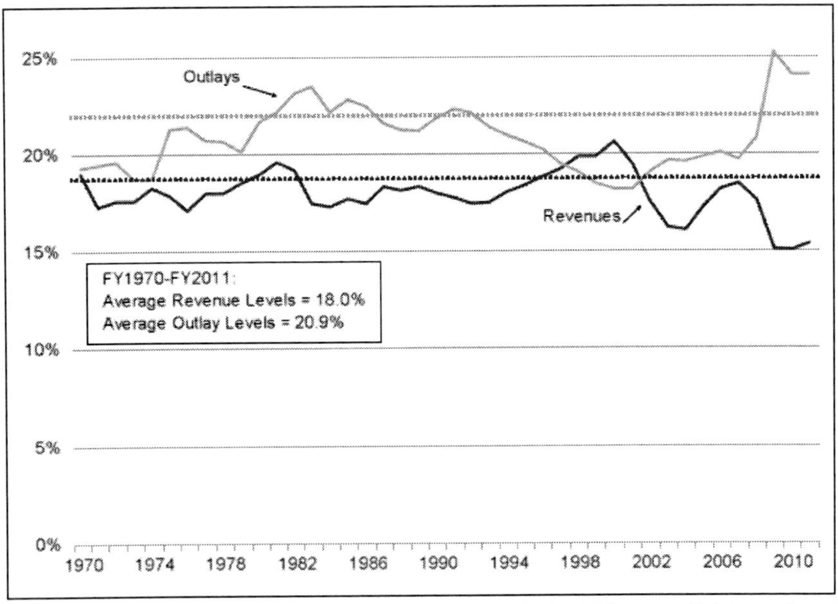

Source: CRS figure using data from CBO, Historical Tables, available at http://www.cbo.gov/doc.cfm?index=12699.

Figure 1. Total Outlays and Revenues, FY1970-FY2011.

Federal Spending

Federal outlays are often divided into the broad categories of discretionary and mandatory spending, and net interest. Discretionary spending is controlled by annual congressional appropriations acts. Mandatory spending encompasses spending on entitlement programs and spending controlled by laws other than annual appropriation acts.[10] Entitlement programs such as Social Security, Medicare, and Medicaid make up the bulk of mandatory spending. Congress sets eligibility requirements and benefits for entitlement programs, rather than appropriating a fixed sum each year. Therefore, if the eligibility requirements are met for a specific mandatory program, outlays are made automatically. Net interest comprises the government's interest payments on the debt held by the public, offset by small amounts of interest income the government receives from certain loans and investments.[11]

In FY2000, total outlays equaled 18.2% of GDP. By FY2011, total outlays reached 24.1% of GDP.[12] Under the CBO baseline, total outlays are projected to be 22.4% of GDP in FY2022. Under CBO's alternative fiscal scenario, outlays are projected to total 24.4% of GDP in FY2022. *Figure 2* shows the level of federal spending as a percentage of GDP, broken into the discretionary, mandatory, and net interest categories, between FY2000 through FY2022, as projected in the CBO baseline.

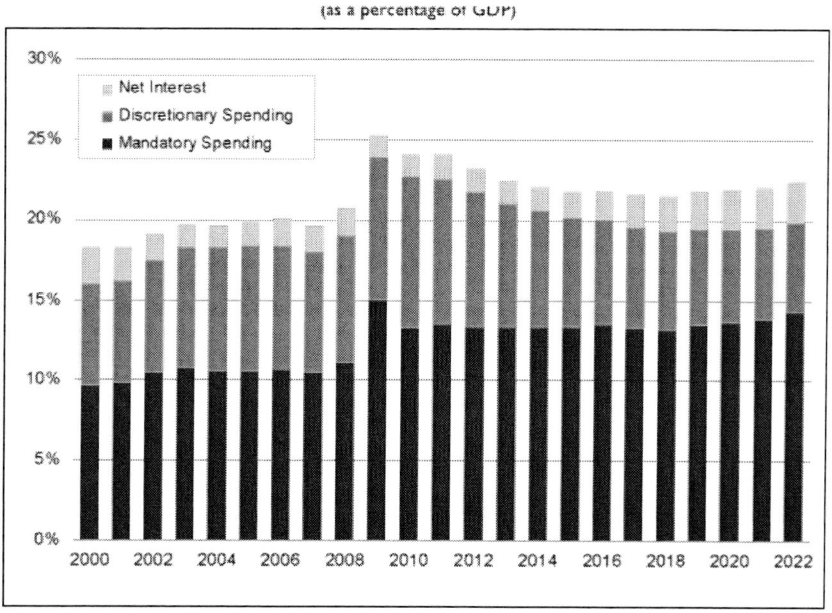

Source: CRS figure using data from CBO, Historical Tables, January 2012.

Notes: Data for FY2012 are estimates and data for FY2013-FY2022 are projections under the current law baseline.

Figure 2. Outlays by Type, FY2000-FY2022.

In FY2011, discretionary spending totaled 9.0% of GDP. Since FY2000, discretionary spending as a share of GDP has increased 7.4% a year, on average, in nominal terms. Increases in discretionary spending over this period have largely been a result of military operations in Iraq and Afghanistan and, more recently, the funding provided in the American Recovery and Reinvestment Act of 2009 (ARRA; P.L. 111-5). On average, from FY2000 to FY2011, defense discretionary outlays grew 8.2% per year in nominal terms, while non-defense discretionary outlays grew 6.6% per year in nominal terms.

By FY2022, according to CBO's baseline projections, discretionary spending will fall to 5.6% of GDP, its lowest level ever.[13]

Mandatory spending totaled 13.5% of GDP in FY2011, up from 9.7% of GDP in FY2000, as shown in *Figure 2*. Mandatory spending levels have been elevated mainly as a result of increases in outlays in income security programs.[14] Though the economic recovery is expected to lower mandatory spending on certain programs over the next few fiscal years, the growth in mandatory spending is projected to resume by the end of the decade due to increases in certain entitlement programs. As a result, under current law, CBO projects that FY2022 mandatory spending will total 14.3% of GDP, higher than the FY2011 level.

In FY2011, mandatory spending totaled 56.3% of total outlays, discretionary spending totaled 37.4% of total outlays, and net interest comprised 6.3% of total outlays. Social Security, Medicare, and the federal share of Medicaid alone constitute 43.4% of all federal spending. Because discretionary spending represents roughly one-third of total federal outlays, some budget experts contend that any significant reductions in federal spending must include mandatory spending cuts. Other budget and social policy experts contend that cuts in mandatory spending would cause substantial disruption to many households, because mandatory spending funds important parts of the social safety net.[15] Nevertheless, there is widespread agreement that action is needed to bring down anticipated high debt and deficit levels to restore long-term fiscal health.[16]

Federal Revenue

In FY2000, revenues equaled 20.6% of GDP. In FY2011, federal revenue collection totaled 15.4% of GDP, one of the lowest levels since FY1950.[17] Revenue collection has remained depressed over the last few fiscal years as the result of the economic downturn and several tax relief provisions. The longer term revenue outlook depends on the speed of economic recovery and the legislative actions of Congress on certain expiring tax provisions and potential tax reform. Under the CBO baseline, revenues are projected to total 21.0% of GDP in FY2022.

The increase in revenue levels in the baseline is largely due to the assumptions that certain tax provisions expire as scheduled under current law, resulting in increases in tax rates and higher revenue collection.[18] Under CBO's alternative fiscal scenario, revenues are projected to total 18.3% of GDP in FY2022.

Individual income taxes have long been the largest source of federal revenues, followed by social insurance (payroll) and corporate income taxes.[19] In FY2011, individual income tax revenues totaled 7.3% of GDP. Payroll tax revenue accounted for 5.5% of GDP20 and corporate income tax revenues equaled 1.2% of GDP in FY2011.

Overall, federal revenues increased very slightly relative to their FY2009 levels. Figure 3 shows revenue collections between FY2000 through FY2022, as projected in the CBO baseline.

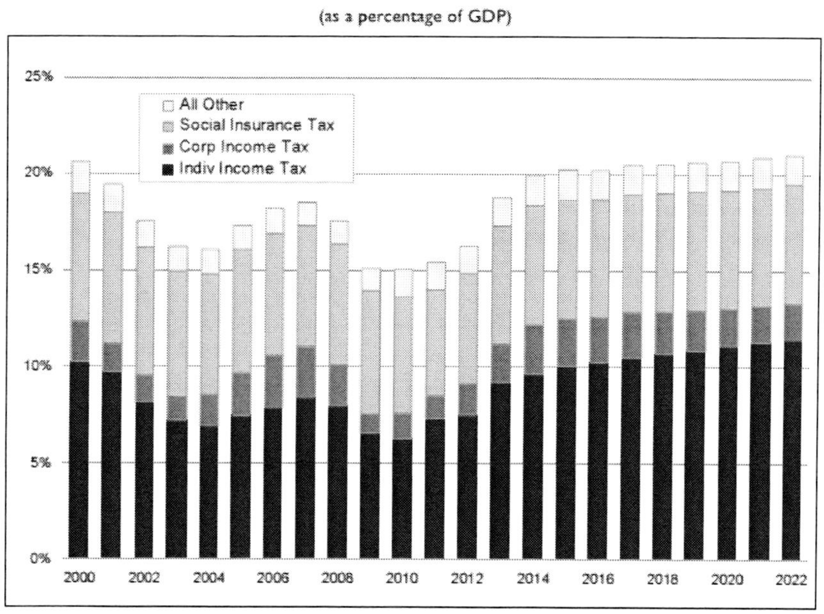

Source: CRS figure using data from CBO, Historical Tables, January 2012.

Notes: Data for FY2012 are estimates and data for FY2013-FY2022 are projections under the current law baseline.

Figure 3. Revenue by Type, FY2000-FY2022.

Deficits, Debt, and Interest

The annual differences between revenue (i.e., taxes and fees) that the government collects and outlays (i.e., spending) result in the budget deficit (or surplus).[21]

Annual budget deficits or surpluses determine, over time, the level of federal debt and affect the growth of interest payments to finance the debt.

Budget Deficits

Beginning with FY2009, annual budget deficits as a percentage of GDP have been sharply higher than deficits in any period since FY1945. The total deficit in FY2011 was $1,296 billion, or 8.7% of GDP. The total deficit, according to some budget experts, gives an incomplete view of the government's fiscal condition because it includes Social Security surpluses (which are held in Treasury trust funds until used to pay future benefits).[22] Excluding off-budget items (Social Security benefits paid net of Social Security payroll taxes collected and the US Postal Service's net balance), the on-budget FY2011 federal deficit was $1,363 billion. The FY2011 total deficit was slightly lower as a percent of GDP than the FY2010 deficit ($1,293 billion or 9.0% of GDP) and lower than the FY2009 deficit ($1,413 billion and 10.1% of GDP).[23]

Occasional deficits, in and of themselves, are not necessarily problematic. Deficit spending can allow governments to smooth outlays and taxes to shield taxpayers and program beneficiaries from abrupt economic shocks in the short term, while also temporarily boosting GDP when the output gap is large. Persistent deficits, however, lead to growing levels of federal debt that may lead to higher interest payments and may also have adverse macroeconomic consequences in the long term, including slowing investment and lowering economic growth. Since the debt cannot grow faster than GDP forever, large deficits will eventually need to be reduced through increases in taxes, reductions in spending, or both.

Federal Debt and Debt Limit

Gross federal debt is composed of debt held by the public and intragovernmental debt.[24] Intragovernmental debt is the amount owed by the federal government to other federal agencies, to be paid by the Department of the Treasury.

This amount largely consists of money contained in trust funds, such as Social Security, that has been invested in federal securities as required by law. Debt held by the public is the total amount the federal government has borrowed from the public and remains outstanding. This measure is generally considered to be the most relevant in macroeconomic terms because it is the debt sold in credit markets.

Changes in debt held by the public generally track the movements of the annual on-budget deficits and surpluses.[25] Whether or not the movements of gross federal debt will follow those of debt held by the public depends on how intragovernmental debt changes.

Congress sets a ceiling on federal debt through a legislatively established limit. The debt limit also imposes a form of fiscal accountability that compels Congress, in the form of a vote authorizing a debt limit increase, and the President, by signing the legislation, to take visible action to allow further federal borrowing when nearing the statutory limit. The debt limit, however, can hinder the Treasury's ability to manage the federal government's finances when the amount of federal debt approaches this ceiling. In those instances, the Treasury has had to take unusual and extraordinary measures to meet federal obligations, leading to inconvenience and uncertainty in Treasury operations at times.[26]

At the end of FY2011 (September 30, 2011), federal debt subject to limit was approximately $14,747 billion, of which $10,127 billion was held by the public.[27] The debt limit currently stands at $16,394 billion, as a result of the provisions of the Budget Control Act of 2011 (P.L. 112-25).[28]

Net Interest

In FY2011, the United States spent $227 billion or 1.5% of GDP on net interest payments on the debt. What the government pays in interest depends on market interest rates as well as on the size and composition of the federal debt. Currently, low interest rates have held net interest payments as a percentage of GDP below the historical average despite increases in borrowing to finance the deficit.[29] Some economists, however, have expressed concern that federal interest costs could rise sharply once the economy recovers, resulting in future strain on the budget.[30] Net interest payments, under the CBO baseline, are projected to rise to $624 billion or 2.5% of GDP in FY2022.

BUDGETING IN TOUGH ECONOMIC TIMES

The economic downturn increased the deficit as a result of elevated levels of spending related to "automatic stabilizers," like unemployment compensation and the Supplemental Nutrition Assistance Program (SNAP), and subsequent policy actions taken by the federal government to address the recession.

Federal spending tied to means-tested social programs has also been increasing due to persistently high levels of unemployment, while federal revenues have fallen as individuals' incomes and corporate profits dropped. The pace of the economic recovery could continue to affect deficit levels.

Federal Responses to the Economic Downturn

The federal government responded to financial turmoil with an extraordinary set of measures in 2008 and 2009, including two major economic stimulus measures and a variety of programs within the Federal Reserve, Treasury, and Federal Deposit Insurance Corporation (FDIC).

In February 2008, Congress enacted a $152 billion package (P.L. 110-185, Economic Stimulus Act of 2008) to stimulate consumption by sending refunds to taxpayers and letting firms depreciate capital investments more quickly. Another effort to jump-start economic growth came in the form of a second stimulus package signed into law by President Obama on February 17, 2009. The American Recovery and Reinvestment Act of 2009 (ARRA; P.L. 111-5) included provisions that are now estimated to total $831 billion in increased discretionary and mandatory spending and reduced tax revenue over the FY2009-FY2019 period. CBO estimates that over 90% of ARRA's direct impact on the deficit will have occurred by the end of FY2011.[31] ARRA contains support for state and local governments in the form of increased transportation project, Medicaid, and school funding; funding for health care information technology; extended unemployment benefits; as well as tax cuts and rebates among other provisions.[32]

In addition to these stimulus efforts, various governmental bodies, through legislative and existing authority, engaged in numerous financial stability programs. These programs included the conservatorship of government-sponsored enterprises Fannie Mae and Freddie Mac and the Emergency Economic Stabilization Act of 2008 (EESA; P.L. 110-343), which authorized the purchase of troubled assets through the Troubled Assets Relief Program (TARP). The Federal Reserve created a variety of lending facilities to provide financial institutions with loans in exchange for various types of collateral. The FDIC used its standing authority to resolve failed banks and administer the federal guarantees on individual deposits, in addition to carrying out a broad guarantee program on debt issued by banks and supporting joint interventions in large banks.[33] Though these financial interventions had significant budgetary impact particularly in FY2009 and FY2010, they are not projected to have a major impact on the budget deficit going forward.

Budget Deficit Estimates for FY2012

The January 2012 CBO baseline estimated the FY2012 budget deficit at $1,079 billion or 7.0% of GDP, lower than the FY2011 (8.7% of GDP) deficit. Spending, though lower than its FY2009 peak, remains several percentage points above the historical average, while receipts remain well below their historical average (see *Figure 1*). The decline in the estimated budget deficit for FY2012, relative to FY2011, is mainly due to increases in tax revenue expected under current law with the expiration of the payroll tax reduction on February 29, 2012 and the deceleration of business tax depreciation for new equipment.

Under the President's budget, deficit estimates for FY2012 amount to $1,327 billion or 8.5% of GDP. This is larger than CBO's baseline deficit estimate primarily due to the cost of short-term measures to stimulate job growth, including an extension of the payroll tax reduction for the entire calendar year, extending long-term unemployment benefits, extending the first-year depreciation deduction for certain property, and providing a temporary tax credit for new jobs.[34]

Budget for FY2013

The Obama Administration released its FY2013 budget on February 13, 2012. Congress has also begun its consideration of the FY2013 budget.

Obama Administration's FY2013 Budget

Consistent with the presentation of previous budgets, the Obama Administration provided three separate deficit projections.[35] First, OMB projected a Budget Enforcement Act (BEA) baseline, using methods that mirror those CBO uses to project its current-law baseline. The BEA baseline assumes that discretionary spending remains constant in real (i.e., inflation-adjusted) terms, the 2001/2003/2010 tax cuts expire at the end of calendar year 2012, and that the alternative minimum tax (AMT) will not be "patched."[36] Many budget analysts believe such projections offer an overly rosy scenario of the long-term budget picture. Under this scenario, the FY2013 deficit is projected to total $598 billion.

The Obama Administration also projected an Adjusted Baseline, which in its view, provides a more transparent and realistic reflection of the federal government's current fiscal situation.[37] They use this methodology as a basis for understanding how new policy choices would affect the fiscal outlook, essentially replacing the current BEA baseline. The Administration's Adjusted Baseline assumes that the 2001/2003/2010 tax cuts will be extended, that the alternative minimum tax (AMT) will be "patched," effectively adjusting the exemption level for inflation, that the estate taxes will be extended at 2011 levels, and the spending limits set in the Budget Control Act are in place. This baseline also includes an adjustment for disaster costs. The deficit under this scenario is projected to reach $772 billion in FY2013.

The final deficit projection, the Proposed Budget, illustrates the impact on the budget outlook if all of the policies of the Obama Administration are implemented. In FY2013, the Administration projects that the deficit will reach $901 billion. Both the Adjusted Baseline and the Proposed Budget project deficits throughout the 10-year budget window. Under the Proposed Budget, the deficit would fall from 5.5% of GDP in FY2013 to 2.7% of GDP by FY2018, before rising to 2.8% of GDP from FY2019 to FY2022.[38]

Generally, the deficit levels in the Proposed Budget scenario fall between the lower BEA baseline and the higher Adjusted Baseline figures. Critics argue that the President's budget makes the deficit worse in the short-term and takes credit for deficit reduction over 10 years that would happen automatically under the baseline.

What Do These Baselines Reflect?

As stated above, the Adjusted Baseline assumes that certain policies due to expire will be continued. The President's budget views the Adjusted Baseline as the most realistic projection of the budget deficit and it is used as their benchmark to measure the impact of their budget proposals. The Proposed Budget, however, is the one that illustrates the resulting budget outlook if all of the policies proposed by the President were implemented. Whether or not a certain policy proposal increases or decreases the deficit depends on which baseline is being used as the starting point.

There are no real limits on what assumptions can be used to construct the Adjusted Baseline as opposed to the BEA baseline whose parameters were set by legislation. The Adjusted Baseline in the FY2013 budget assumes, for example, costly increases in the deficit to "patch" the AMT and continue the 2001/2003/2010 tax cuts. Because these policies serve to increase the deficit, the Administration can show decreases in the deficit by measuring its Proposed Budget against this constructed Adjusted Baseline, rather than against the BEA baseline. For example, because the Administration assumes a full continuation of the 2001/2003/2010 tax cuts in its Adjusted Baseline, at a cost of $2,173 billion between FY2013 and FY2022, their proposal included in the Proposed Budget to allow the tax cuts on top income earners to expire, results in a "savings" of $1,433 billion over the same period. However, relative to the BEA baseline, the extension of the tax cuts increases the deficit by $740 billion.[39]

A similar methodology can be used in understanding how the AMT "patch" is being accounted for in each baseline. The Adjusted Policy baseline incorporates an annual AMT "patch" at 2011 parameters, which increases the deficit by $1,898 billion over the FY2013-FY2022 period relative to the BEA Baseline. Because this proposal is already included in the Adjusted Baseline, it does not have any additional deficit impact in the Proposed Budget, which maintains the "patch."

Major FY2013 Budget Proposals

In his budget for FY2013, President Obama presented his policy agenda, largely focused on providing additional stimulus to create jobs and bolster the economic recovery while operating within the discretionary spending limits currently in law. The main policy initiatives he emphasized include various spending and tax proposals, as well as longer term deficit reduction. The budget also emphasizes continued investment in and reform of education and job training programs as well as a continued push for research and development incentives and infrastructure improvements. Overall, the proposed budget cuts the deficit in half, in dollar terms (and as a percentage of GDP) by the middle part of the decade. However, the deficit begins to rise again in the second half of the decade.

The President's budget proposes a variety of tax and spending measures aimed at job creation, largely drawn from the American Jobs Act submitted to Congress in September 2011. These proposals amount to nearly $350 billion in additional spending and tax cuts, including immediate funding for roads, rails and runways, aid to states and local governments for teachers and first responders, school modernization and a full-year extension of the Social Security payroll tax reduction and unemployment benefits. Of this funding, approximately $178 billion is expected to be spent in FY2012 and $137 billion in FY2013, with smaller amounts in later years.

While the President proposes additional stimulus that increases the deficit in the short term, he also includes a package of spending cuts and revenue increases to reduce the deficit over the next 10-years. In August 2011, the Budget Control Act (BCA) placed limits on spending via discretionary spending caps and included provisions for additional spending cuts in the amount of $1.2 trillion (for more information see the section titled "Budget Control Act of 2011"). In January 2013, the additional cuts are scheduled to take effect via an automatic process. In his FY2013 budget, President Obama proposes replacing the automatic cuts with prescribed spending cuts and tax increases. The largest of these proposals include allowing the 2001/2003/2010 tax cuts for singles making over $200,000 and households making over $250,000 to expire, savings generated from changes to Medicare, Medicaid, agriculture, and other mandatory programs, and placing caps on spending on Overseas Contingency Operations (OCO).[40] Together, these deficit reduction proposals total $1,992 billion.[41]

The budget proposal also included other tax proposals changes in the estate tax parameters, limits the value of itemized deductions for married taxpayers with incomes over $250,000 and single taxpayers with incomes over $200,000, and eliminates various tax expenditures.[42] The Administration also released a framework for corporate tax reform, which included a reduction in the corporate tax rate combined with an elimination of certain corporate tax expenditures. The Administration is committed to reform that would not add to the deficit.[43]

Finally, the President's Budget also includes a *Cuts, Consolidations, and Savings* volume that contains proposed changes to 210 discretionary and mandatory programs, which could save approximately $24 billion in FY2013 if enacted.[44]

Longer term budgetary challenges remain the biggest driver of fiscal challenges. These challenges are partially addressed by a variety of budget proposals. However, further programmatic reforms, beyond those laid out in the budget proposal, will likely be needed to fully address these longterm deficit drivers.

Congressional Consideration of the FY2013 Budget Resolution

The House and Senate Budget Committees are responsible for formulating and reporting an annual budget resolution. The budget committees typically develop the budget resolution as they receive information and testimony from various sources, such as the Administration, CBO, and congressional committees with jurisdiction over spending and revenues. The timetable established in the Congressional Budget Act directs the Senate Budget Committee to report a budget resolution by April 1, and for the House and Senate to reach final agreement on a budget resolution by April 15.[45]

On March 21, 2012, the House Budget Committee reported the budget resolution (H.Con.Res. 112, 112th Congress) by a vote of 19-18. The resolution provided for revenue levels of $2,734 billion and outlays of $3,530 billion in FY2013 for a deficit of $797 billion, or approximately 5.0% of GDP. By FY2022, the deficit is projected to fall to $287 billion or 1.2% of GDP. Debt held by the public is projected to rise in nominal terms from $12,261 billion in FY2013 to $15,364 billion by FY2022.[46]

The budget proposal contains changes to both spending and revenue. The Budget Control Act specified a statutory cap on discretionary spending of $1,047 billion for FY2013. Under the House budget resolution, top line discretionary spending for FY2013 would be further reduced to $1,028 billion. Like the President's budget proposal, the House budget resolution specifies a replacement of the Budget Control Act's automatic cuts, scheduled to take place in January 2013, with spending cuts to be achieved elsewhere. The budget resolution contains reconciliation instructions to six committees to find further deficit reduction of $261 billion over 10 years. Though the committee report accompanying the budget resolution does contain preferred policy options by which to achieve these savings, the committee has the authority to report whatever changes it wants within its jurisdiction in response to the reconciliation directive. Policy options from the budget committee include changes to federal health programs, the Supplemental Nutrition Assistance Program, job training and education programs, and the federal workforce. Under this proposal, overall government spending would be reduced to the historical average of roughly 20% of GDP by FY2015.

On the revenue side, the Budget Committee, in the report accompanying the budget resolution, suggests replacing the current system with two tax brackets of 10% and 25% and repealing the Alternative Minimum Tax. The corporate tax rate would also be reduced from 35% to 25%. To offset the reduction in tax rates, certain tax expenditures would be eliminated in order to broaden the base of taxable income. Revenue collection would average roughly 18% of GDP between FY2013 and FY2022 under this proposal.

Because the budget resolution does not become law, separate legislation would have to be enacted in order to make some of the policy changes that are relied upon in the proposal. The budget proposal does not contain specifics on how some of the revenue and spending proposals would be achieved. Therefore, if some of the policy proposals do not become law, the spending, revenue, and deficit projections could change significantly. Further affecting deficit levels are the economic assumptions used in making any budget projections. The House budget resolution uses CBO's January 2012 estimates, which are roughly in line with those in the President's budget.[47] If economic growth is higher or lower, the deficit levels and related components in the budget resolution would be affected.

The Senate Budget Committee has not yet considered a budget resolution for FY2012.

CONSIDERATIONS FOR CONGRESS

Congress faces ongoing budgetary challenges in FY2013 with both short-run and long-run budget priorities that may conflict in critical ways. In the short term, economic issues may continue to dominate the policy debates. In addition, Congress will have to make decisions in several key policy areas. Over the long term, increasing federal health care costs are expected to keep mandatory spending rising, placing ever-increasing focus on how to achieve fiscal sustainability.

Addressing the Budget Deficit

Over the next several months, Congress is expected to discuss several revenue and spending policies that, if changed from current law, could have a large impact on the size of the budget deficit going forward.

Tax Provisions

On December 17, 2010, the Tax Relief, Unemployment Insurance Reauthorization, and Job Creation Act of 2010 (P.L. 111-312) was signed into law.

This legislation had numerous provisions, including the extension of the 2001 and 2003 ("Bush") tax cuts until the end of 2012, reinstating the estate tax until the end of 2012, and "patching" the alternative minimum tax until the end of 2011. Under the law, long-term unemployment benefits were also extended and the employee portion of the Social Security payroll tax was cut by two percentage points until the end of 2011. Relative to current law, CBO estimated that the spending and revenue measures in the bill would increase the deficit by $390 billion in FY2011 and by $468 billion over the FY2012-FY2020 period, with nearly all the impact on the deficit occurring between FY2011 and FY2013.[48]

The payroll tax reduction, long-term unemployment benefit extension, and "doc fix" were extended for two months, through February 29, 2012, as part of Temporary Payroll Tax Cut Continuation Act of 2011 (P.L. 112-78). These measures were extended through the end of calendar year 2012 as part of Middle Class Tax Relief and Job Creation Act of 2012 (H.R. 3630). CBO estimates that this legislation, enacted as part of H.R. 3630, will increase the deficit by $89.3 billion over the FY2012-FY2022 period.[49]

Budget Control Act of 2011

On August 2, 2011, the President signed into law the Budget Control Act of 2011 (BCA; P.L. 112- 25).[50] The BCA contained a variety of measures intended to reduce the deficit by at least $2.1 trillion over the FY2012-FY2021 period, along with a mechanism to increase the debt limit. The deficit reduction provisions included $917 billion in savings from statutory caps on discretionary spending and the establishment of a Joint Select Committee on Deficit Reduction (Joint Committee) to identify further budgetary savings of at least $1.2 trillion over 10 years. On November 21, 2011, the co-chairs of the Joint Committee announced that they were unable to reach an agreement before the committee's deadline. As a result, a $1.2 trillion automatic spending reduction process has been triggered to begin in January 2013 unless Congress and the President act to eliminate or change the process before then. While the BCA is projected to reduce the deficit, it does not eliminate budget deficits or growth in the federal debt over the 10- year budget window.

Even with the deficit reduction contained in the BCA, many budget analysts believe that additional savings are required to put the budget on a sustainable path over the long-term, particularly if some of the policies set to expire under current law are, instead, continued. (See earlier discussion in the section "Budget Baseline Projections".) Even under the current law baseline, which includes the BCA's $2.1 trillion in deficit reduction, projected deficits of $3.1 trillion over 10 years remain.

Other Short-Term Considerations

The economy is still recovering from the most recent recession, which lasted from December 2007 to June 2009. Conditions remain weak, in part, due to budget challenges facing state and local governments, high levels of consumer debt, and continuing weakness in many real estate markets. Most economists expect unemployment rates to remain elevated for the medium term. During this period, the budget deficit grew largely as a result of government actions taken to combat the economic downturn as well as significantly lower revenue and higher spending levels directly attributable to the economic conditions.

As the economy continues to recover, revenue should increase as unemployment falls and spending should decrease due to less reliance on federal programs meant to provide assistance during economic downturns. This should lead to decreases in the budget deficit relative to current levels in the short term. Though many argue that fiscal stimulus and other actions were needed to help the economy recover, the resulting large budget deficits and high debt levels will have an effect for many years.

Many budget analysts are concerned about future levels of federal debt and acknowledge that the current spending and revenue collection cannot continue at current or projected future levels. However, making significant changes to spending or revenue policies at this time may be harmful to the ongoing economic recovery. On the other hand, the longer that the country continues without a plan to stabilize its fiscal future, the more costly reform may be. In addition, the likelihood of a severe fiscal crisis caused by an unwillingness of private investors to continue financing unsustainable deficits may increase, and if that occurs, reforms may be forced by events, rather than being well planned.[51]

General Budget Issues

Congress may wish to consider some general budgeting issues beyond these short-term considerations.

Budget Transparency

The budget, reflecting the size and complexity of the federal government, is complicated and detailed. The budget books that OMB compiles provide an enormous amount of information, and other budget data reported by federal agencies provide even more detail on federal spending plans. The Federal Funding Accountability and Transparency Act of 2006 (P.L. 109-282) included several measures to increase the accessibility of budget information. For example, as a result of that act, OMB now runs the USAspending.gov website, which provides detailed information on federal spending. Concerns have been raised about the quality of those data.[52] Moreover, it is not clear that those data are thoroughly coordinated with other federal budgeting data systems.

Congress and the President have undertaken additional efforts in an attempt to improve transparency in light of the large amounts of spending currently occurring as a result of economic stabilization efforts and federal financial interventions. For example, Recovery.gov was launched to track stimulus spending. The Congressional Oversight Panel was established in the Emergency Economic Stabilization Act to oversee TARP spending. Despite this, criticisms remain and requests for greater transparency continue.

In certain cases, despite the large amount of data provided by OMB and other government agencies, it can be difficult to answer relatively simple budget questions. Critics maintain that the federal government in general and OMB in particular should take steps to make data on federal spending even more transparent to taxpayers and more useful to policymakers. Even as the President's budget mentions "a new tracking tool" to provide daily updates on spending by agency, Congress may wish to consider requiring these changes to provide more organized and transparent budget data to citizens and to itself.[53]

Long-Term Considerations

Budget deficits or surpluses are not always the best indication of long-term fiscal stability. Most economists agree that, under certain conditions, running a budget deficit may be necessary to provide economic stimulus or pull an economy out of recession. A large budget deficit in a single year, in itself, does not necessarily indicate a longer term problem. The federal government, however, does face serious long-term budget challenges. Some measures of fiscal solvency in the long term indicate that, under current policy, the US may face a major future crisis, specifically as it relates to rising health care costs and the likely impact on government-financed health care spending.

CBO, GAO, and the Administration agree that the current mix of federal fiscal policies is unsustainable in the long term. The nation's aging population, combined with rising health care costs per beneficiary, seems likely to keep federal health costs rising faster than per capita GDP. CBO projected in June 2011 that under current policy, federal spending on federal health programs (including Medicare, Medicaid, CHIP, and exchange subsidies) would grow from 5.6% of GDP today to 10.3% of GDP in 2035, and to nearly 20% by 2085.[54] The 2010 Economic Report of the President also called the trajectory of future federal spending on Medicare and Medicaid unsustainable.[55] GAO's recent long-term fiscal simulations, under an alternative policy scenario, projected debt held by the public as a share of GDP to exceed the post World War II historical high in about 15 years.[56]

Keeping future federal outlays at 20% of GDP, or approximately at its historical average, and leaving fiscal policies unchanged, according to CBO projections, would require drastic reductions in all spending other than that for Medicare, Social Security, and Medicaid, or reining in the costs of these programs. Under the extension of current law, CBO estimates that the nation's current fiscal gap, a present-value measure of fiscal imbalance for a given time period, would reach 0.2% of GDP over the next 75 years. This means that an immediate and permanent reduction in spending, increase in revenues, or a combination of spending cuts and revenue increases amounting to 0.2% of GDP would be needed to make the government's debt the same size (relative to the size of the economy) at the end of that period as it was at the beginning.

Under an alternative fiscal scenario, which incorporates policy changes that are widely expected to occur and that policymakers have regularly made in the past, the fiscal gap reaches 8.3% of GDP.[57] This indicates that an immediate and permanent reduction in spending, increase in revenues, or a combination of spending cuts and revenue increases amounting to 8.3% of GDP would be needed to make the government's debt the same size (relative to the size of the economy) at the end of that period as it was at the beginning.[58] In other words, to ensure a sustainable fiscal path over the next 75-years where debt remains at the same level of GDP as it is currently, spending would have to be immediately and permanently cut by 31%, revenue would have to be increased by 44%, or some combination of the two.

As the economic recovery continues, Congress may focus more effort on balancing the budget and reining in the debt. This would require less spending, increases in revenue collections, faster-than-average economic growth, or a combination of these things. Debt requires interest payments that can strain budgets if debt levels and interest rates are high. High debt levels could limit the government's flexibility in meeting its obligations or in responding to emerging needs of its citizens. Ultimately, failing to take action to reduce the projected growth in the debt potentially might lead to future insolvency or government default.[59]

Appendix. Budget Documents

CBO Documents

The Congressional Budget Office (CBO) provides data and analysis to Congress throughout the budget and appropriations process. Each January, CBO issues a *Budget and Economic Outlook* that contains current-law baseline estimates of outlays and revenues.

In March, CBO typically issues an analysis of the President's budget submission with revised baseline estimates and projections. In late summer, CBO issues an updated *Budget and Economic Outlook* with new baseline projections.

In these documents, CBO sets a current-law baseline as a benchmark to evaluate whether legislative proposals would increase or decrease outlays and revenue collection. Baseline estimates are not intended to predict likely future outcomes, but to show what spending and revenues would be if current law remained in effect. CBO typically evaluates the budgetary consequences of legislative proposals and the Joint Committee on Taxation (JCT) evaluates the consequences of revenue proposals.

CBO also releases other periodic publications focusing on the future fiscal health of the United States. In their publication, *The Long-Term Budget Outlook*, CBO makes projections on the state of the federal budget to FY2083. They discuss spending and revenue levels and the related issues that they expect will arise under different policy assumptions. In their *Budget Options* volumes, they provide specific policy options and the impact they will have on spending and revenues over a 10-year budget window. They also provide arguments for and against enacting each policy.

OMB Documents

The President's Budget typically contains six volumes: (1) *The Budget*; (2) *Historical Tables*; (3) *Analytical Perspectives*; (4) *Appendix*; (5) *Terminations, Reductions, and Savings*; and (6) *Supplemental Materials*.[60] These documents lay out the Administration's projections of the fiscal outlook for the country, along with spending levels proposed for each of the federal government's departments and programs. The *Historical Tables* volume also provides significant amounts of budget data, much of which extends back to 1962 or earlier. Along with the Administration's budget documents, the Department of the Treasury also releases its *Green Book*, which provides further detail on the revenue proposals that are contained in the budget.[61]

End Notes

[1] For more information, see CRS Report 98-721, *Introduction to the Federal Budget Process*, coordinated by Bill Heniff Jr.

[2] Congressional Budget Office, Estimated Impact of the American Recovery and Reinvestment Act on Employment and Economic Output from July 2011 Through September 2011, November 2011, p. 2; US Congress, US House of Representatives Committee on Financial Services, Federal Reserve programs to strengthen credit markets and the economy,

Testimony of Federal Reserve Chairman Ben S. Bernanke, February 10, 2009, available at http://www.federalreserve.gov/newsevents/testimony/bernanke20090210a.htm.

[3] Unless stated otherwise, data used in this report are from Congressional Budget Office, *The Budget and Economic Outlook: Fiscal Years 2012 to 2022*, January 2012, available at http://cbo.gov/publication/42905.

[4] For more information on the BCA, see CRS Report R41965, *The Budget Control Act of 2011*, by Bill Heniff Jr., Elizabeth Rybicki, and Shannon M. Mahan and CRS Report R42013, *The Budget Control Act of 2011: Effects on Spending Levels and the Budget Deficit*, by Marc Labonte and Mindy R. Levit.

[5] CRS Report 98-325, *The Federal Fiscal Year*, by Bill Heniff Jr.

[6] The contents of the Presidential budget submission are governed by 31 USC. §1105. For reasons why the budget may be delayed, see CRS Report RS20179, *The Role of the President in Budget Development*, by Bill Heniff Jr.

[7] Congress does not always complete action on a budget resolution. In years when Congress is late in adopting, or does not adopt, a budget resolution, the House and Senate independently may adopt "deeming resolution" provisions for the purpose of enforcing certain budget levels. The last time Congress agreed to a budget resolution was for FY2010. The FY2010 budget resolution was agreed to on April 29, 2009. For more information, see CRS Report RL30297, *Congressional Budget Resolutions: Historical Information*, by Bill Heniff Jr. and Justin Murray and CRS Report RL31443, *The "Deeming Resolution": A Budget Enforcement Tool*, by Megan Suzanne Lynch.

[8] For more information on the appropriations and authorization process, see CRS Report 97-684, *The Congressional Appropriations Process: An Introduction*, by Jessica Tollestrup.

[9] Many of the rules governing the baseline, contained in §257 of the Balanced Budget and Emergency Deficit Control Act, as amended, were extended or modified as part of the Budget Control Act of 2011 (P.L. 112-25).

[10] For more information on trends in discretionary and mandatory spending, see CRS Report RL34424, *Trends in Discretionary Spending*, by D. Andrew Austin and Mindy R. Levit and CRS Report RL33074, *Mandatory Spending Since 1962*, by D. Andrew Austin and Mindy R. Levit.

[11] Net interest is discussed in further detail below in the section "Deficits, Debt, and Interest."

[12] Total outlays peaked at 25.2% of GDP in FY2009.

[13] The division between discretionary and mandatory spending was first put into place in FY1962.

[14] Mandatory spending peaked in FY2009 at 15.0% of GDP.

[15] For more information, see CRS Report R41970, *Addressing the Long-Run Budget Deficit: A Comparison of Approaches*, by Jane G. Gravelle and CRS Report R41778, *Reducing the Budget Deficit: Policy Issues*, by Marc Labonte.

[16] In various reports, the Congressional Budget Office, the Government Accountability Office, and the Administration agree that the federal government's budget is on an unsustainable path. For more information, see the section of this report titled, "Long-Term Considerations."

[17] In FY2009 and FY2010, revenue collection totaled 15.1% of GDP.

[18] For more information, see CRS Report R41591, *Tax Reform: An Overview of Proposals in the 112th Congress*, by James M. Bickley.

[19] For more information, see CRS Report RL32808, *Overview of the Federal Tax System*, by Molly F. Sherlock and Donald J. Marples.

[20] Payroll tax revenue has declined over the last fiscal year largely due to a reduction in the employee payroll tax rate from 6.2% to 4.2%, which began on January 1, 2011.

[21] Most economists use data on federal outlays to track larger budget trends, while most program analysts use budget authority to track changes in specific program areas.

[22] From an overall budget perspective, these surpluses are used to offset other federal spending, thereby decreasing the current budget deficit while increasing the amount of Treasury securities held in the Trust Fund.

[23] US Office of Management and Budget, *Budget for Fiscal Year 2013*, *Historical Tables*, Table 1-3, available at http://www.whitehouse.gov/omb/budget/Historicals/.

[24] Gross federal debt is also referred to as total debt or total public debt outstanding. Intragovernmental debt is also referred to as intragovernmental holdings or debt held by federal government accounts.

[25] In FY2009 and FY2010, the increase in the deficit was larger than that of debt held by the public due to the nature of the obligations incurred as a result of the government conservatorship of Fannie Mae and Freddie Mac and the TARP program.

[26] General Accountability Office, *Delays Create Debt Management Challenges and Increase Uncertainty in the Treasury Market*, GAO-11-203, February 2011.

[27] US Office of Management and Budget, *Budget for Fiscal Year 2012*, *Historical Tables*, Tables 7-1 and 7-2.

[28] For further details, see CRS Report RL31967, *The Debt Limit: History and Recent Increases*, by D. Andrew Austin and Mindy R. Levit.

[29] Since FY1970, the US spent an average of 2.2% of GDP on interest payments.

[30] Carmen M. Reinhart and Kenneth S. Rogoff, "The Aftermath of Financial Crises," *American Economic Review*, vol. 99 (2009), no. 2, p. 10; Alan Auerbach and William Gale, "The Economic Crisis and the Fiscal Crisis: 2009 and Beyond An Update," Tax Policy Center, September 2009, available at http://www.taxpolicycenter.org/UploadedPDF/ 1001284_ economic_crisis.pdf.

[31] The cost estimate for ARRA has changed since it was originally projected due to revised economic and technical assumptions and certain legislative changes. See source for additional notes. US Congressional Budget Office, *The Budget and Economic Outlook: Fiscal Years 2012 to 2022*, January 2012, Box 1-1.

[32] For more information on the provisions of ARRA, see CRS Report R40537, *American Recovery and Reinvestment Act of 2009 (P.L. 111-5): Summary and Legislative History*, by Clinton T. Brass et al.

[33] For more information, see CRS Report R41073, *Government Interventions in Response to Financial Turmoil*, by Baird Webel and Marc Labonte.

[34] Office of Management and Budget, *Budget for Fiscal Year 2013*, *The Budget*, Tables S-2 and S-9.

[35] For details of these projections, see US Office of Management and Budget, *Budget for Fiscal Year 2012*, *The Budget*, Tables S-1 (Proposed Budget) and S-7 (BEA Baseline and Adjusted Baseline).

[36] The tax cuts were enacted in the Economic Growth and Taxpayer Relief Act of 2001 (EGTRRA; P.L. 107-16) and the Jobs and Growth Tax Relief Reconciliation Act of 2003 (JGTRRA; P.L. 108-27) and extended as part of The Tax Relief, Unemployment Insurance Reauthorization, and Job Creation Act of 2010 (P.L. 111-312). For more information, see CRS Report R42020, *The 2001 and 2003 Bush Tax Cuts and Deficit Reduction*, by Thomas L. Hungerford.

[37] In prior years, this scenario had been known as the Current Policy Baseline.

[38] US Office of Management and Budget, *Budget for Fiscal Year 2013, The Budget*, Tables S-4 and S-6. In March 2012, CBO estimated that the President's Proposed Budget would result in a deficit of $977 billion or 6.1% of GDP in FY2013. By FY2022, CBO projects a deficit of $728 billion or 3.0% of GDP based on the President's proposals. Congressional Budget Office, *An Analysis of the President's 2013 Budget*, Table 1.

[39] These figures do not include related debt service costs or savings.

[40] OCO spending is currently exempt from the BCA discretionary spending caps. Part of the savings would be used to invest in a six-year surface transportation reauthorization package. Whether or not savings can be generated by reducing OCO spending from current levels has been controversial. For CBO's take on the issue, see Congressional Budget Office, Director's Blog, *Can Proposed Reductions in Future War-Related Spending Be Used To Offset Proposed Deficit Increases in Other Areas?*, February 1, 2012.

[41] The deficit reduction proposed in the President's budget to replace the automatic spending reduction process total $3,187 billion. However, the budget also proposes to cancel the $1,195 billion automatic process cuts. Therefore, the cumulative effect of these reductions is $1,992 billion. CRS calculations based on Office of Management and Budget, *Budget for Fiscal Year 2013, The Budget*, Table S-2.

[42] For full detail on the revenue proposals included in the President's budget, see Department of the Treasury, *General Explanations of the Administration's Revenue Proposals (Green Book)*, February 2012.

[43] The White House and the Department of the Treasury, *The President's Framework for Business Tax Reform*, p. 1, February 2012.

[44] Office of Management and Budget, *Budget for Fiscal Year 2013, Cuts, Consolidations, and Savings*, p. 1.

[45] For more information on the congressional budget process, see CRS Report RS20368, *Overview of the Congressional Budget Process*, by Bill Heniff Jr.

[46] US House of Representatives, Committee on the Budget, The Path to Prosperity: A Blueprint for American Renewal, Table S-1.

[47] US House of Representatives, Committee on the Budget, H.Rept. 112-421, p. 26 and Table 6.

[48] Between FY2014 and FY2020, the legislation is estimated to reduce the deficit by $59 billion. Congressional Budget Office, *The Budget and Economic Outlook: Fiscal Years 2011 to 2021*, January 2011, Box 1-1.

[49] Congressional Budget Office, *Budgetary Effects of the Conference Agreement for H.R. 3630, the Middle Class Tax Relief and Job Creation Act of 2012, as Posted on the Web Site of the House Committee on Rules on February 16, 2012*. For more information, see CRS Report R42103, *Extending the Temporary Payroll Tax Reduction: A Brief Description and Economic Analysis*, by Donald J. Marples and Molly F. Sherlock and CRS Report RL33362, *Unemployment Insurance: Programs and Benefits*, by Katelin P. Isaacs and Julie M. Whittaker.

[50] For more information on the Budget Control Act of 2011, see CRS Report R41965, *The Budget Control Act of 2011*, by Bill Heniff Jr., Elizabeth Rybicki, and Shannon M. Mahan and CRS Report R42013, *The Budget Control Act of 2011: Effects on Spending Levels and the Budget Deficit*, by Marc Labonte and Mindy R. Levit.

[51] Congressional Budget Office, *Federal Debt and the Risk of a Fiscal Crisis*, July 27, 2010, p. 1.

[52] For more information, see CRS Report RL34718, *The Federal Funding Accountability and Transparency Act: Implementation and Proposed Amendments*, by Garrett Hatch.

[53] Office of Management and Budget, *Budget for Fiscal Year 2011, The Budget*, p. 44.

[54] Congressional Budget Office, *The Long-Term Budget Outlook*, June 2011, pp. 45-46 and "Supplemental Material."

[55] Council of Economic Advisors, *Economic Report of the President*, February 2010, p. 140.

[56] Government Accountability Office, *The Federal Government's Long-Term Fiscal Outlook: Fall 2011 Update* (GAO12-28SP), October 23, 2011, p. 1.

[57] The alternative fiscal scenario includes things like the extension of certain expiring tax provisions and the continued indexation of AMT to inflation through 2021 and Medicare physician payment rates are maintained at 2011 levels through 2021 and not restrained thereafter by policies in current law. For a complete description of the assumptions included in the extended baseline and alternative fiscal scenarios, see Congressional Budget Office, *The Long-Term Budget Outlook*, June 2011, Table 1-1.

[58] US Congressional Budget Office, *The Long-Term Budget Outlook*, June 2011, Table 1-3.

[59] See Alan Auerbach and William Gale, "The Economic Crisis and the Fiscal Crisis: 2009 and Beyond: An Update," Tax Policy Center working paper, September 2009, available at http://www.brookings.edu/~/media/Files/rc/papers/ 2009/06_fiscal_crisis_gale/06_fiscal_crisis_gale_update.pdf.

[60] The President's budget proposals can be found on the OMB website at http://www.whitehouse.gov/omb/. The Supplemental Materials include the Federal Credit Supplement, the Object Class Analysis, the Balances of Budget Authority, and the Public Budget Database.

[61] The Green Book is available at http://www.treasury.gov/resource-center/tax-policy/Pages / general_explanation.aspx.

In: The Federal Budget: 2013 and Beyond ISBN: 978-1-62081-920-3
Editors: J. Lambert and I. Johnson

Chapter 2

REDUCING THE BUDGET DEFICIT: POLICY ISSUES*

Marc Labonte

SUMMARY

In 2009, the federal budget deficit (the difference between outlays and revenues) exceeded $1 trillion for the first time, and it has remained above $1 trillion since. Those years also marked the largest the deficit has been as a share of gross domestic product (GDP) in the period since World War II. The budget is not projected to be on a sustainable path under current policy, in the sense that it leads the publicly held debt to continuously grow more quickly than GDP. The timing of deficit reduction remains a difficult issue because of continued weakness in the economy.

If deficits are reduced too quickly, the economy might tip back into recession. If unsustainable deficits persist for too long in the economic recovery, it could crowd out private investment and, in the worst case scenario, investors could refuse to continue to finance deficits that they believed were unsustainable.

As one example of the policy changes that would return the budget to a sustainable path, the Congressional Research Service (CRS) estimates that stabilizing debt as a share of GDP at its 2011 level would require

---

* This is an edited, reformatted and augmented version of a Congressional Research Service publication, CRS Report for Congress R41778, from www.crs.gov, prepared for Members and Committees of Congress, dated February 15, 2012.

budget deficits averaging 2.8% of GDP over the next 10 years. In dollar terms, the deficit could equal $200 billion in 2013, rising to more than $600 billion from 2015 on.

Under the Congressional Budget Office's (CBO's) current law baseline, the deficit is already on a sustainable path. Under CBO's Alternative Fiscal Scenario, which modifies the current law baseline by assuming that expiring tax provisions and the "doc fix" to Medicare are extended and that the future automatic spending cuts under the Budget Control Act (BCA) do not come into effect, the deficit would decline from more than 9% of GDP in 2011 to 5% of GDP in 2015, then rise to 6% of GDP by 2022. To reduce the deficit to sustainable levels under this scenario would require some combination of spending cuts and tax increases equivalent to roughly $800 billion in 2013, falling to $275 billion in 2015, then rising to $900 billion by 2022.

The recent growth in deficits is the result of spending reaching its highest level as a share of GDP since 1945 and revenues reaching their lowest level as a share of GDP since 1950. Revenues were low because of the recession and because of the temporary extension of expiring tax provisions, such as the "alternative minimum tax (AMT) patch" and "Bush tax cuts."

If these tax cuts are extended again, revenues are estimated to be reduced by about 2.5% of GDP from 2014 on and will remain around their historical average from 2015 on.

Thus far, policy changes to reduce the deficit have targeted mainly discretionary spending. The BCA would reduce discretionary spending by $1.5 trillion and mandatory spending by less than $0.2 trillion over 10 years if automatic cuts are allowed to begin in 2013. Including interest savings, the BCA would reduce the deficit by about 1% of GDP from 2014 on.

Even if these cuts proceed as scheduled, overall spending is projected to rise and remain above its historical average over the next 10 years because of the growth in mandatory spending. Defense, Social Security, and Medicare account for more than half of total spending. Outside of those three programs and net interest, all other spending is about three-quarters the size of the budget deficit in 2012.

Growth in entitlement spending on the elderly drives long-term projections of large budget deficits—by mid-century, outlays on Social Security and health programs would exceed total revenues. Most proposals to reform entitlement programs for the elderly would generate significant budgetary savings in the long run, but little budgetary savings in the short run, partly because most proposals exempt current retirees from reform and partly because the savings from these changes would compound over time.

The US fiscal outlook is not a purely long-term issue, however—deficits are already at unsustainably high levels today.

INTRODUCTION

The federal budget has been in deficit (i.e., spending has exceeded revenues) since 2002, and deficits became significantly larger in 2009. That year, the deficit topped $1 trillion for the first time ever, and it is projected to remain above $1 trillion in 2012 for the fourth year in a row.[1] Relative to the overall size of the economy, budget deficits from 2009 to 2011 have been significantly larger than in any other year since World War II.

From 1946 to 2008, budget deficits averaged 1.7% of gross domestic product (GDP) and exceeded 5% of GDP only three times (equaling 7.2% in 1946, 6.0% in 1983, and 5.1% of GDP in 1985). From 2009 to 2011, the budget deficit averaged 9.3% of GDP, and it is projected to equal 7% of GDP in 2012.[2] Current deficits are larger as a share of GDP than any recorded historically except for those recorded during the Civil War, World War I, and World War II. In the past, deficits have proven sustainable because periods of moderate growth in the debt relative to GDP have been followed by periods when debt fell relative to GDP. Under current policy, deficits are projected to cause the federal debt to continuously grow faster than national income, which is unsustainable. The federal debt held by the public has grown from 40% of GDP in 2008 to a projected 73% of GDP in 2012.

Congress has expressed interest in examining policy options to reduce the deficit. The Congressional Research Service (CRS) does not take a position on the best way to reduce the deficit. This report organizes and presents information to help policymakers frame the debate. This report first discusses the size of projected budget deficits, then discusses how much the deficit would need to be reduced to return to long-term sustainability, then analyzes alternative time frames for reducing the deficit, and finally discusses broad policy choices for reducing the deficit.

WHAT POLICY CHANGES HAVE BEEN TAKEN TO REDUCE THE DEFICIT SO FAR?

From FY2001 to FY2010, policy changes added to budget deficits each year.[3] In FY2011, policy changes were a mix of deficit-reducing legislation and deficit-increasing legislation. To date, recent policy steps to reduce the deficit have primarily focused on reducing discretionary spending (i.e., spending that is provided and controlled through the appropriations process).

Discretionary outlays declined from $1.347 trillion in 2010 and $1.346 trillion in 2011 to a projected $1.308 trillion in 2012. Part of that decline is caused by a decline in spending on overseas contingency operations (OCO), but most is the result of a decline in non-defense discretionary spending. Because inflation reduces the purchasing power of $1 over time, the decline is larger in real terms. Relative to the January 2011 baseline level, which adjusts for inflation, discretionary spending was reduced by $29 billion in 2011.[4]

The reduction in 2011 discretionary spending occurred through the 2011 appropriations process. For 2012 to 2021, the Budget Control Act (P.L. 112-25) reduced discretionary spending and mandatory spending were reduced relative to the baseline.[5] The Budget Control Act cut spending through a two-step process.[6] In the first step, student loan programs were cut and statutory caps were set for discretionary spending for 2012 to 2021, with OCO, disaster spending, and emergency spending exempt from the caps. In the second round (often referred to as the "trigger"), additional spending cuts will be implemented beginning in January 2013. Most of these round two spending cuts will fall on discretionary spending, through sequestration (the across-the-board cancellation of budgetary resources) in 2013 and a reduction to the statutory discretionary caps for 2014 to 2021. Most mandatory programs are exempted from the act's cuts, but a few smaller programs and parts of Medicare that are not will be cut through a sequestration from 2013 to 2021. The cut to Medicare is capped at 2%.

Relative to 2011 levels adjusted for inflation, CBO projects that the Budget Control Act reduces defense discretionary spending by $15 billion in 2012 and $812 billion over 10 years and nondefense discretionary spending by $12 billion in 2012 and $714 billion over 10 years.[7] These estimates require some assumption to be made about the levels of discretionary spending that will occur in categories that are exempt from the caps. For example, CBO assumes that emergency spending, which is exempted from the caps and designated by Congress and the President, will be zero in the next 10 years; if emergency spending does take place, discretionary savings from the Budget Control Act would be reduced dollar for dollar. In addition, the Budget Control Act cuts mandatory spending on student loan programs by $5 billion over 10 years and cuts other mandatory spending (mostly Medicare) through the second-round sequester by $165 billion over 9 years.[8] Since lower outlays would result in a lower debt relative to the baseline, debt service savings from these spending cuts would reduce the deficit by roughly another $300 billion over 10 years. Including these interest savings, the Budget Control Act reduces the annual deficit by about 1% of GDP from 2014 on.

If Congress acts to prevent the second round of spending cuts from taking place beginning in January 2013, but leaves the first round discretionary caps in place, total discretionary spending would be reduced by $778 billion over 10 years. In this scenario, mandatory spending would be cut by only $5 billion, with the cuts falling on student loan programs.

Although spending has been cut, other policy goals, such as stimulating the economy, have also led to recent policy changes that have increased the deficit relative to the baseline. For example, CBO estimates that the Tax Relief, Unemployment Insurance Reauthorization, and Job Creation Act of 2010 (P.L. 111-312) increased the deficit by $374 billion in 2011, of which $204 billion is attributable to the extension of expiring tax provisions. This act extended the "Bush tax cuts" [9] for two years, extended the alternative minimum tax (AMT) "patch" for one year,[10] extended and expanded unemployment benefits for one year, and implemented a one year payroll tax cut. The 112th Congress has debated whether each of these provisions should be allowed to expire as scheduled or extended further and whether further extensions should be deficit-financed or offset by spending cuts or other tax increases.

How Large Are Projected Deficits Under Current Policy?

Absent policy changes, budget deficits would change over time because spending and revenue levels automatically change over time. Baseline budget projections are used to provide a benchmark against which budgetary decisions can be made and policy proposals can be compared over the budget window. A baseline is not meant to be the best guess of future outcomes or the most desirable outcome, but a reasonable starting point for comparing policy options. The projected magnitude and path of budget deficits depends greatly on what baseline assumptions are made.

CBO estimates an official 10-year *current law* baseline, which assumes that certain provisions of law will expire as scheduled, even though many of these provisions have routinely been extended in the past.[11] Examples of such provisions include the 2001 and 2003 tax cuts (popularly known as the "Bush tax cuts"), which were extended until the end of 2012 to avoid their expiration at the end of 2010, and the "alternative minimum tax (AMT) patch," which has been repeatedly extended, most recently until the end of 2011. Another example is the Medicare cuts required in law by the sustainable growth physician payment formula; Congress has enacted legislative overrides to prevent those cuts (popularly known as the "doc fix") each year since 2003.[12] CBO's current law baseline also assumes that the second round of spending cuts under the Budget Control Act will occur in 2013 as scheduled. Under the current law baseline, the deficit would decline to about 1% of GDP by 2017, mostly due to the baseline assumptions that the Bush tax cuts and AMT patch will be allowed to expire as scheduled.

CBO also presents an unofficial Alternative Fiscal Scenario, which is a *current policy* baseline that assumes that spending and revenue policies in place now would remain in place. The Alternative Fiscal Scenario modifies the current law baseline by assuming that the doc fix[13] and all expiring tax provisions are extended (including the Bush tax cuts and the AMT patch, as well as dozens of smaller "extenders," with the exception of the payroll tax cut). It also assumes that the second round spending cuts in the Budget Control Act "trigger" will not come into effect in 2013 as scheduled, although it assumes that the first round discretionary caps will remain in place. It yields much larger budget deficits, because the policy changes raise outlays or lower revenues and because the larger budget deficits increase the interest that must be paid on the national debt.

Table 1 illustrates deficit projections under various scenarios, starting with the current law baseline and ending with the Alternative Fiscal Scenario. Under the Alternative Fiscal Scenario, the deficit would bottom out at 5.1% of GDP in 2015. It would then begin to rise again, and reach 6.1% of GDP by the end of the projection window. From 2017 on, the deficit under the Alternative Fiscal Scenario is more than four times larger than the current law baseline relative to GDP. The extension of the Bush tax cuts and AMT patch adds $5.4 trillion to the deficit over 10 years, more than the effects of all of the other assumptions made in the Alternative Fiscal Scenario combined.[14]

Discretionary spending poses conceptual problems for baseline projections. Baseline projections are attempting to extrapolate current policy, not predict the most likely outcome. Because it is determined on an annual basis, there is more than one reasonable assumption of what could be considered an extension of "current policy" into the future. In its baseline projection, CBO assumes that discretionary spending will match the levels set by the Budget Control Act. But the Budget Control Act only sets certain types of discretionary spending in statute; it sets no limit on overseas contingency operations (OCO) or any emergency spending, as designated by Congress and the President.

Table 1. Deficit Projections Under Alternative Assumptions
Fiscal Year

	2012	2013	2014	2016	2017	2018	2019	2020	2021	2022	
				billions of dollars							
CBO Current Law	$1,079	$585	**$345**	$269	$302	$220	$196	$258	$280	$279	$339
Baseline											
Baseline + "Doc Fix"	$1,088	$604	$366	$293	$330	$252	$233	$301	$330	$334	$401
Baseline + "Doc Fix" +	$1,100	$683	$483	$399	$427	$346	$328	$398	$432	$443	$518
Extenders											
Baseline + "Doc Fix" +	$1,111	$916	$822	$794	$869	$841	$880	$1,014	$1,117	$1,201	$1,357
Extenders + Extend											
"Bush Tax Cuts" and											
"AMT Patch"											
CBO Alternative Fiscal	$1,111	$981	$917	$899	$981	$960	$1,005	$1,144	$1,253	$1,344	$1,495
Scenario											
				% of GDP							
CBO Current Law	7.0%	3.7%	2.1%	1.5%	1.6%	1.1%	0.9%	1.2%	1.2%	1.2%	1.4%
Baseline											
Baseline + "Doc Fix"	7.0%	3.8%	2.2%	1.7%	1.8%	1.3%	1.1%	1.4%	1.5%	1.4%	1.6%
Baseline + "Doc Fix" +	7.1%	4.3%	2.9%	2.3%	2.3%	1.8%	1.6%	1.8%	1.9%	1.9%	2.1%
Extenders											
Baseline + "Doc Fix" +	7.2%	5.8%	5.0%	4.5%	4.6%	4.3%	4.3%	4.7%	4.9%	5.1%	5.5%
Extenders + Extend											
"Bush Tax Cuts" and											

Table 1. (Continued)

	2012	2013	2014	2016	2017	2018	2019	2020	2021	2022	
				billions of dollars							
"AMT Patch"											
CBO Alternative Fiscal	7.2%	6.2%	5.5%	5.1%	5.2%	4.9%	4.9%	5.3%	5.5%	5.7%	6.1%
Scenario											

Source: CRS calculations based on CBO data.

Notes: Cost of alternative policy assumptions includes additional debt service generated by those assumptions.CBO Alternative Fiscal Scenario = Baseline + "Doc Fix" + Extenders + Extend "Bush Tax Cuts" and "AMT Patch" + BCA Trigger. See text for details.

In the baseline, CBO assumes that OCO spending will increase at the rate of inflation and emergency spending will be zero.[15] Altering those assumptions would result in higher or lower projections of baseline spending under current law. Prior to enactment of the Budget Control Act, CBO assumed that discretionary spending would increase at the rate of inflation (i.e., would stay constant in real terms)—an assumption that was lower than historical growth rates. Under this assumption, deficits would be nearly one percentage point of GDP larger by the end of the 10-year budget window.

Budget projections are subject to a high degree of uncertainty—based on history, actual outcomes are likely to be much better or worse than projections. OMB estimates that the absolute average errors for its budget deficit projections are 1.5% of GDP for the next budget year and 3.5% of GDP for five years in the future.[16] This implies that maintaining the status quo (under the "current policy" baseline) could lead to a successful return to sustainability in five years, or to sustainability problems that are more serious than current projections would suggest.

WHY ARE DEFICITS PROJECTED TO DECLINE?

As *Table 1* illustrates, much of the projected reduction in the deficit over the next 10 years is a function of the assumptions made by the current law baseline. But even the Alternative Fiscal Scenario projects that the deficit will fall from over 9% of GDP in 2009-2011 to 7% of GDP in 2012 to as low as 4.9% of GDP in 2017. The deficit declines under the Alternative Fiscal Scenario for the following reasons:

- CBO projects that revenues automatically rise and certain mandatory spending automatically falls as the economy eventually returns to full employment. Economists refer to these changes as "automatic stabilizers." Assuming all expiring tax provisions are extended, revenues are projected to rise from about 15% of GDP in 2011 to 18% of GDP from 2017 on.[17] By 2015, unemployment compensation is projected to fall to less than half of its 2011 level in nominal dollars, although this is partly due to the expected expiration of the temporary extension of benefits.
- The temporary spike in budget authority caused by the American Reinvestment and Recovery Act (ARRA, P.L. 111-5, popularly known as the 2009 "Economic Stimulus Act") has dissipated. ARRA

was intended to be only a temporary boost to spending to stimulate the economy, and Congress has allowed budget authority to return to close to pre-ARRA levels to date.[18]

- Most financial stabilization outlays in the federal budget occurred within the Troubled Asset Relief Program (TARP)[19] or on transfers to the government sponsored enterprises (GSEs). CBO projects that there will be only minimal outlays on financial stabilization programs going forward, due to improvements in financial markets and the expiration in 2010 of Treasury authority to enter into new contracts with regards to TARP and the GSEs. In 2009, outlays of $243 billion were recorded for TARP and the GSEs. In 2010 and 2011, transfers to the GSEs declined and, due to budgetary conventions, TARP recorded negative outlays that reduced the deficit.[20]
- CBO assumes in the Alternative Fiscal Scenario that discretionary spending will adhere to the first round discretionary caps created by the Budget Control Act. This would reduce discretionary spending from 9% of GDP in 2011 to 6% of GDP in 2022, which would be its lowest level since data were first collected in 1962.

The projected decline in deficits is temporary, under any scenario in *Table 1*, and is followed by a gradual, long-term increase in the projected deficit. Long-term projections indicate that budget deficits would eventually become very large relative to GDP outside the projection window under current policy if revenues remain similar to their historical share of GDP. Under a long-term projection of current policy, CBO projects deficits would exceed 10% of GDP by 2026 and 20% of GDP by 2043.[21]

How Much Deficit Reduction Is Necessary?

The targeted amount of deficit reduction depends on the policy goal. A balanced budget could be pursued so that the government would have a neutral effect on the national saving rate (by accounting identity, budget deficits reduce the national saving rate).[22] Since the United States has a low national saving rate relative to other countries and relative to domestic investment needs, a case could be made that the government should at least not continue to reduce the national saving rate by running budget deficits in the future. If the policy goal were for the government to increase the national saving rate or reduce the federal debt, then the government could target a budget surplus.

Some economists call for a balanced structural budget, which would allow for modest deficits in downturns and budget surpluses in boom times. For 2009 to 2011, a structurally balanced budget would have allowed for an actual deficit of about 21/4% of GDP.[23]

A less ambitious policy goal would be to return fiscal policy to a sustainable path. History demonstrates that budget deficits can be sustained indefinitely as long as they are small enough that government debt does not continuously grow more quickly than GDP. The budget is not projected to be on a sustainable path under current policy (as defined by the Alternative Fiscal Scenario) because the debt held by the public would continuously grow more quickly than GDP, reaching 94% of GDP in 2022, thus implying that an ever-growing portion of national income would be needed to meet interest payments. As long as investors remain willing to finance large deficits, there is no barrier to the debt continuing to grow relative to GDP, and there has been no difficulty in financing it to date. At some point, however, investors would refuse to continue to finance such deficits, because the proportion of national income devoted to interest payments cannot rise indefinitely.[24] The size of the deficit compatible with sustainability depends on the size of the debt at the time it is stabilized and projected GDP growth rates. Because it is unknown how much longer the debt can be increased relative to GDP, for illustrative purposes, CRS estimates the budget deficits that would be consistent with stabilizing debt as a share of GDP at its projected 2012 level (73% of GDP) based on CBO's projections of GDP growth. Stabilizing the debt at 2012 levels would require annual budget deficits no larger than approximately 1% of GDP in 2013, rising to 3.5% of GDP in 2015 and 2016, falling to 2.75% of GDP from 2019 on.[25] In dollar terms, this would amount to a deficit of about $175 billion in 2013, rising to the $600 billion range from 2015 on. If actual policy followed the current law baseline, the budget deficit is already projected to be on a sustainable path. Compared with the Alternative Fiscal Scenario in *Table 1*, achieving sustainability would require some combination of spending cuts and tax increases equivalent to roughly $800 billion in 2013, falling to $275 billion in 2015, and rising each year thereafter until it exceeds $900 billion by 2022. In other words, one possible path to fiscal sustainability is to allow the policy changes already scheduled in law to occur. Another possible path is to prevent those changes from occurring, and then make offsetting cuts in spending or increases in taxes of $800 billion in 2013. CRS makes no recommendations on the best set of policies to achieve sustainability.

Under CBO's Alternative Fiscal Scenario and current interest rate projections, net interest on the federal debt is larger than the sustainable budget deficit, meaning that revenues would need to exceed non-interest spending (what economists call a "primary surplus") to stabilize the debt relative to GDP. Were GDP growth lower or interest rates higher than projected, the primary surplus would have to be larger to be sustainable, and vice versa. By historical standards, CBO's projections of economic growth over the next 10 years are relatively modest, but this is mostly because CBO projects that the labor supply will grow much more slowly than it has historically due to the aging of the population. Projections assume that interest rates will remain at relatively low levels by historical standards over the next 10 years. CBO estimates that if interest rates rose to their average level from 1991 to 2000, the budget deficit would be an average of $100 billion higher per year over the next 10 years. If interest rates rose to their average level from 1981 to 1990, the budget deficit would be an average of $500 billion higher per year over the next 10 years.[26]

Because deficits are projected to continue to grow in the long run, growing cuts in spending or increases in taxes would be required over time to maintain sustainability. Larger cuts in spending or increases in taxes would be required today to spread those changes evenly over time. For example, CBO projects that spending would need to be cut or revenues increased by 8.3% of GDP immediately to stabilize the debt-to-GDP ratio over the next 75 years, which would result in a projected budget surplus in 2012.[27]

The US fiscal outlook is not a purely long-term issue, however—deficits are already at unsustainably high levels today, and while projected deficits are larger than today's deficits outside the 10-year budget window, they are also more uncertain. The deficit is a long-term issue in that the economic consequences from running large deficits have been minor to date, but there is the risk that that the deficit's effect on the economy could become negative, possibly acutely so, at any time. Deficits are also a long-term issue in the sense that most observers believe fundamental reforms to outlays and revenues would be necessary to put the budget on a sustainable path; however, any delay to implementing those changes increases the eventual budgetary cost of returning to a sustainable fiscal path, all else equal.

How Quickly Should the Deficit Be Reduced?

The state of the economy is an important factor to consider in determining the desired timing of deficit reduction. All else equal, mainstream economic theory predicts that reducing the deficit would have a contractionary effect on the economy in the short run, whether it be through tax increases or spending reductions. During a period of robust economic growth, that contractionary effect would be more easily absorbed by other sectors of the economy, and the expansion would likely be sustained. During a period of high unemployment, such as the present, reducing the budget deficit would be expected to make unemployment higher (or fall more slowly) than would otherwise be the case, all else equal. On these grounds, an argument could be made for postponing deficit reduction until the economy improves. Given that the effect on the economy is proportional to the size of the deficit reduction, avoiding unwanted contractionary effects also argues for a gradual approach to deficit reduction.

On the other hand, the risk of a fiscal crisis as long as the deficit is at an unsustainable level would argue for moving to sustainability as quickly as possible to eliminate that risk. Low interest rates indicate that markets believe there is little risk of a crisis currently, but market sentiment can change quickly, as has occurred in countries such as Greece and Ireland. In these countries, GDP has contracted deeply and unemployment has risen sharply.

CBO projects that unemployment will rise to 9% in 2013 and 2014. These economic projections are based on the CBO "current law" baseline deficit, which is reduced rapidly between 2012 and 2013. Under the Alternative Fiscal Scenario, which projects a more gradual reduction in the deficit, CBO projects that unemployment would be between 7.4% and 8.9% in 2013. Nevertheless, CBO projects that significant deficit reduction under the current law baseline would not prevent the eventual return to full employment by 2017.

POLICY OPTIONS FOR DEFICIT REDUCTION

Budget deficits can be reduced through cuts in spending, higher taxes, or a combination of both. Plans to reduce the deficit are faced with the fact that Social Security, Medicare, and defense make up more than half of total spending. *Figure 1* compares the projected deficit to overall spending and revenues in FY2012. It shows that the deficit is about three-quarters the size of all non-interest spending outside of Social Security, Medicare, and defense discretionary. It is also more than three-quarters of total discretionary spending (defense and non-defense combined). It is about half the size of total revenues.

Budget deficits are the result of the shortfall between spending and revenue. As seen in *Figure 2*, spending in 2009 reached its highest level as a share of GDP since 1945 and revenues have reached their lowest level as a share of GDP since 1950.

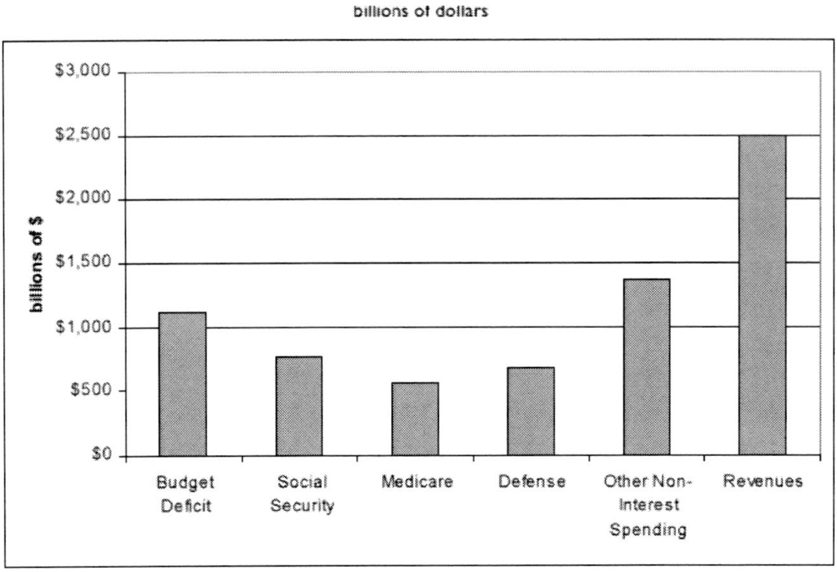

Source: CRS calculations based on CBO data.

Note: Budget deficit, spending, and revenues for 2012 are projected based on the January CBO baseline.

Figure 1. Selected Data from FY2012 Federal Budget.

From 1946 to 2008, outlays averaged 19.6% of GDP, and were generally below 20% of GDP until 1975, above 20% of GDP from 1975 to 1996, and below 20% of GDP from 1997 to 2005. From 2009 to 2011, outlays averaged 24.1% of GDP.

From 1946 to 2008, revenues averaged 17.8% of GDP, showing no long-term upward or downward trend from 1952 to 2007. Revenues were at least 17% of GDP in each year during that period except for 1955, 1959, 2003, and 2004, when they were between 16% and 17%. From 2009 to 2011, revenues were below 16%.

Just as recent deficits are the combination of all past outlay and revenue decisions, returning the budget to balance would be difficult without a combination of outlay and revenue changes.

For instance, to return the budget to balance while maintaining 2011 revenue levels would require that outlays decline to a share of GDP last seen in the 1950s.

Likewise, to balance the budget while maintaining 2011 outlay levels would require revenues to rise to their highest share of GDP ever.

1946-2022

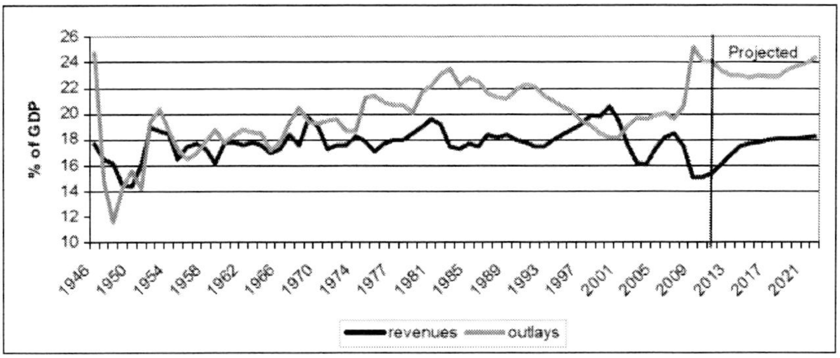

Source: OMB and CRS calculations based on CBO data.
Notes: See Table 1 for details on the Alternative Fiscal Scenario.

Figure 2. Federal Revenues and Outlays, Historical and Projected Under the Alternative Fiscal Scenario.

Federal Spending

Total spending under the Alternative Fiscal Scenario would fall by nearly one percentage point of GDP from 2011 to 2012, and is projected to average 23.4% of GDP in the 10-year budget window. (Total spending under the CBO current law baseline never falls below 21.5% of GDP.) From 1946 to 2008, there were only three years when outlays were above 23% of GDP. By 2022, total spending is projected to exceed its 2011 share of GDP under the Alternative Fiscal Scenario—despite discretionary spending falling to its lowest share of GDP since data was first collected—because mandatory spending and net interest on the federal debt grow relative to GDP. The projected increase in net interest is due to the growth in the federal debt and the return to more normal interest rates from the below-average rates currently prevailing.

Discretionary Spending

Large budget deficits relative to GDP since 2009 have corresponded with higher levels of discretionary spending relative to GDP, but not historically high levels since data was first available in 1962, as seen in *Figure 3*. Defense discretionary spending was higher from 1962 to 1992 as a share of GDP than it was in 2010. From 1963 to 2001, defense discretionary spending generally fell relative to GDP—but not in terms of nominal dollars. It then began to grow, when overseas military operations expanded. It currently remains well below the share of GDP that prevailed before the 1990s. Non-defense discretionary spending has shown no long-term upward or downward trend relative to GDP—except for an elevated period from 1975 to 1981, it has always stayed within 3.5% to 4.0% of GDP. Over the late 1990s, it fell to its lowest level of GDP since data has been collected, and then rose from that low base in the 2000s. It has been above its long-term average since 2009, but below the levels prevalent from 1975 to 1981. Since 2009, much of the growth in non-defense discretionary spending was a result of the 2009 Economic Stimulus Act. Most discretionary spending under this act will be completed by 2011.

1962-2022

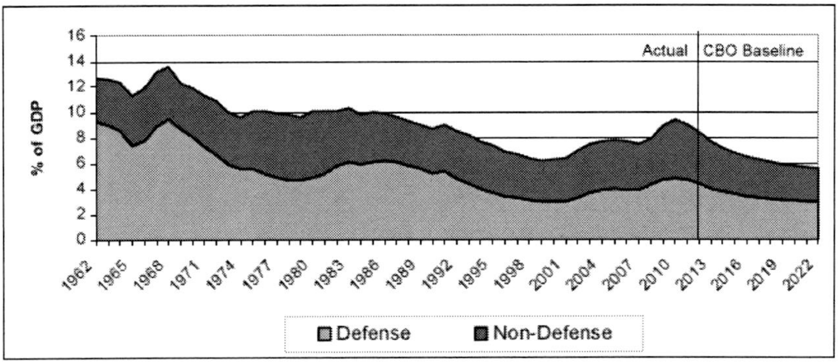

Source: OMB and CBO.

Note: Figure assumes that spending cuts under the Budget Control Act will occur as scheduled.

Figure 3. Discretionary Spending, Historical and Projected in the Baseline.

In the current law baseline, discretionary spending declines significantly relative to GDP over the next 10 years to its lowest share of GDP since data were first collected in 1962, as shown in *Figure 3*. The current law baseline assumes that discretionary spending will adhere to the levels set in the Budget Control Act. Even if the Budget Control Act's automatic "trigger" cuts are not implemented in 2013, total discretionary spending under the discretionary caps would still fall to its lowest share of GDP since 1962.

The CBO current law baseline assumes discretionary spending will fall in nominal terms (i.e., not adjusted for inflation) each year from 2011 to 2015. From 1963 to 2010, discretionary spending fell in nominal terms in only four years, most recently in 1996. Adjusted for inflation, the CBO baseline assumes that both defense and non-defense spending would fall in real terms each year from 2011 to 2022. If this occurred, it would mark a significant break from past policy, as shown in *Table 2.*

Table 2. Average Annual Real Growth Rates of Discretionary Spending Outlays. Actual and CBO Baseline, Adjusted for Inflation

	Defense	Non-Defense
2000-2008	5.1%	3.0%
2009-2010	5.7%	11.4%
2011-2022	-2.4%	-3.2%

Source: CRS calculations based on OMB and CBO data.

Notes: Data for 2000 to 2011 are actual; data for 2012 to 2022 assume that spending cuts under the Budget Control Act will occur as scheduled.

CBO includes the continuation of spending on overseas military operations at current levels (about $146 billion a year in 2012 dollars) in its baseline projection of discretionary spending throughout the 10-year budget window because it is exempt from the Budget Control Act caps. For defense, the timing and magnitude of any potential drawdown in overseas military operations could cause military spending to decline relative to the baseline, but traditionally such changes have not been motivated by deficit reduction. Even if current operations are reduced, future geopolitical events could require military personnel to be deployed elsewhere in the next 10 years, so the baseline does not necessarily overestimate future defense spending.

One macroeconomic implication of reducing discretionary spending is that most federal spending on physical capital (e.g., infrastructure) and human capital (e.g., education) is located in the discretionary portion of the budget. Economic theory predicts that a lower future capital stock would reduce the long-term size of the economy from what it otherwise would be, all else equal.[28]

In long-term projections, CBO holds discretionary spending constant as a share of GDP because it is determined annually. Because discretionary spending is held constant, it is not responsible for the growth of the budget deficit in long-term projections.

Mandatory Spending

Unlike discretionary spending, mandatory spending grew rapidly from 5% of GDP in 1962 to a range of 9% to 10.5% of GDP from 1975 to 2007, peaking in recession years because of automatic stabilizers. It exceeded 13%

of GDP from 2009 to 2011, marking its highest share of GDP since data were first compiled in 1962. In contrast to discretionary spending, mandatory spending is projected to continue to grow faster than inflation and exceed 13% of GDP over the next ten years under current policy. Since 1962, mandatory spending fell in nominal terms in only one year, 2010; if TARP and deposit insurance, which recorded negative outlays that year, are removed, all other mandatory spending grew in 2010.

Over the long term, the upward trend in mandatory spending in the past and future is dominated by Social Security, Medicare, and Medicaid, which accounted for about three-quarters of total mandatory spending in 2010. Between 2007 and the 2009 to 2011 period, the growth in mandatory spending was dominated by financial crisis programs, the 2009 Economic Stimulus Act spending, and automatic stabilizers (primarily located in the Income Security category).

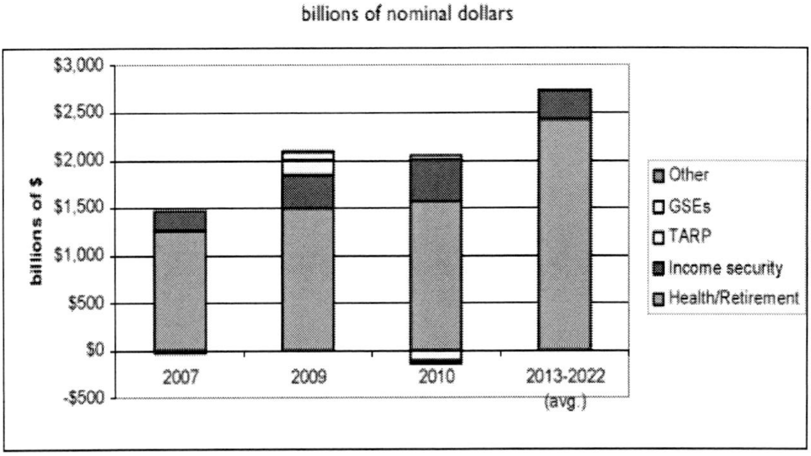

Source: CRS calculations based on CBO data.

Notes: Health/Retirement = Social Security, Medicare, Medicaid, Civil Service and Military Retirement, Veterans, and other health programs (net of offsetting receipts); GSEs = Government Sponsored Enterprises; TARP = Troubled Asset Relief Program; Income Security = unemployment benefits, means-tested transfer programs to households, refundable tax credits; Other = remaining programs net of offsetting receipts. Outlays can be negative for a category because offsetting receipts exceed spending or because of subsidy reestimates for credit programs. Totals for joint state-federal programs include only the federal share.

Figure 4. Mandatory Spending in Selected Years.

From 2007 to 2009, mandatory health and retirement programs (including Social Security, Medicare, and Medicaid) increased by $234 billion or 19%, as shown in *Figure 4*. Over the same period, income security outlays increased by $146 billion or 73%. In FY2009, TARP was created and the GSEs began to receive financial assistance, adding $152 billion and $91 billion to mandatory spending, respectively.

Outside of health and retirement programs, outlays on other mandatory programs are projected to decline significantly in nominal terms over the next 10 years. TARP registered negative outlays of $110 billion in 2010 and $37 billion in 2011, representing downward revisions of the previously estimated cost of the program, and is projected to record outlays of less than $1 billion per year over the next 10 years. Transfers to the GSEs declined to $5 billion in 2011, and are projected to average $3 billion per year over the next 10 years. As the economy improves, "automatic stabilizer" spending is also projected to decline: spending on income security programs more than doubled in nominal terms between 2007 and 2010, but is projected to decline from $438 billion in 2010 to an annual average of $302 billion over the next 10 years.

In long-term budget projections, rising budget deficits are driven primarily by the growth in entitlement programs for the elderly, particularly health spending. Social Security outlays are projected to rise from 4.8% of GDP today to 6.1% of GDP in 2035, and federal health outlays (mainly on Medicare and Medicaid) are projected to rise from 5.6% today to as much as 10.3% of GDP in 2035. By 2050, outlays on Social Security and health programs would exceed total revenues. In part, this growth is driven by the assumptions that go into these projections— revenues and discretionary spending are assumed to stay constant relative to GDP in the long run, whereas health spending per capita is projected to continue to grow faster than GDP per capita because it has historically grown much more quickly. If health spending per capita grew at the same rate as GDP per capita (technically, this is referred to as an excess cost growth rate of zero), much of the increase in federal spending would be avoided, although spending would still grow somewhat because of demographic changes—namely, the retirement of the baby boomers—that increased the number of recipients.[29]

The growth in elderly entitlement spending keeps deficits unsustainably large in the long run. Restraining the future growth rate of this spending would keep the deficit from growing, but it alone would not reduce the budget deficit in the short run. In effect, since the debt is already growing faster than GDP today, restraining elderly entitlement growth would keep the debt to GDP ratio on its current upward—and therefore, unsustainable—trajectory.[30] Most proposals to reform elderly entitlement programs would generate significant budgetary savings in the long run, but little budgetary savings in the short run, partly because most proposals exempt current retirees from reform and partly because the savings from these changes would compound over time. For example, immediately reducing excess cost growth for federal health spending to zero would reduce federal spending by 2% of GDP after 14 years, but by 0.7% of GDP after 5 years.[31]

Revenues

In 2009 and 2010, revenues were at historically low shares of GDP across all major categories— individual income taxes were at their lowest share of GDP since 1950, corporate income taxes were at their lowest share of GDP since the 1930s, social insurance receipts were at their lowest share of GDP since the 1970s, and excise taxes were at their lowest share of GDP since 1934, the first year for which data are available. In recent years, most revenues have come from the individual and social insurance categories. In 2011, income tax revenue rose as a share of GDP because of the economic recovery, but social insurance receipts declined as a share of GDP because of the payroll tax cut (P.L. 111-312), and total revenues remained below historical averages as a share of GDP.

Revenues in the CBO "current law" baseline are projected to exceed 20% of GDP from 2015 on, which is higher than the historical average. This increase occurs primarily because CBO assumes that the "Bush tax cuts" and "AMT patch" expire as scheduled in current law. If the tax cuts and AMT patch continue to be extended (as assumed in the Alternative Fiscal Scenario), revenues would be about 2% of GDP lower in 2014, rising to 2.5% of GDP by 2021. In this scenario, total revenues would gradually increase relative to GDP over the next 10 years due to the improvement in the economy (initially) and "real bracket creep," returning to their historical average around 2014. Real bracket creep refers to the fact that the same tax structure generates more revenue relative to GDP when incomes rise. But revenues would not return to 18.5% of GDP, which is the highest share of GDP that revenues have reached since the Bush tax cuts were fully implemented, at any point in the next decade under the Alternative Fiscal Scenario because of the enactment of additional tax cuts since then.

If policymakers decided to increase revenue to reduce the deficit, five broad choices are often discussed[32]:

- redesigning the structure of the tax system;
- adding new revenue sources, such as a carbon tax or a value added tax (VAT);
- increasing existing taxes;
- "broadening the tax base" by eliminating tax expenditures (deductions, exemptions, and credits); or
- allowing tax cuts to expire as scheduled.

Redesigning the tax system or adding new revenue sources could theoretically improve economic efficiency and might be more appealing to some than increasing existing taxes, but in practice, pressure to compensate those made worse off from these changes may result in those policies raising little additional revenue. Generally, economists favor eliminating tax expenditures over raising marginal tax rates on efficiency grounds, although some specific expenditures may promote economic efficiency. Tax expenditures have also been criticized on the grounds of equity and complexity.[33]

For long-term projections, defining revenues under current policy is problematic. Under current law, revenues are projected to gradually rise relative to GDP over the next 75 years because some parts of the tax system, notably the AMT, are not indexed for inflation and other parts of the system would experience "real bracket creep."[34] If current policy were instead considered to be defined as setting revenues at current levels or returned to historical levels, revenues would be insufficient to match the long-term growth in spending under current policy, and progressively larger budget deficits would result.

CONCLUSION

Budget deficits have reached historically high and unsustainable levels since 2009 because spending has been at its highest share of GDP since 1945 and revenues have reached their lowest share of GDP since 1950. By 2017, deficits decline to about 1% of GDP—a sustainable level in the sense that it would cause the federal debt to fall relative to GDP—under the official CBO "current law" baseline. This baseline makes several assumptions that would mark a significant change from current policy—that tax provisions such as the Bush tax cuts and AMT patch would be allowed to expire as scheduled although they have already been extended at least once, that cuts to Medicare physician payments would be allowed although Congress has routinely prevented those cuts, and that discretionary spending will fall to historically low shares of GDP under the Budget Control Act. Under CBO's Alternative Fiscal Scenario, budget deficits under a continuation of current policy (as opposed to current law) would remain between 5% and 6% of GDP and would continually rise as a share of GDP after 2014 over the next 10 years.

One policy goal is to place the deficit on a sustainable path so that the publicly held debt stabilizes as a share of GDP. For illustrative purposes, CRS estimates that to stabilize the debt as a share of GDP at its projected 2012 level (73% of GDP) would require average annual budget deficits of 2.8% of GDP over the next 10 years. In dollar terms, this would amount to a deficit of about $400 billion in 2012, rising to about $550 billion in 2015. Compared with the "current policy" baseline, this would require some combination of spending cuts and tax increases equivalent to more than $700 billion in 2012 and $400 billion in 2015.

Balancing the budget through changes to one subsection of the budget is not mathematically possible at 2012 levels. For example, total spending outside of Social Security, Medicare, defense, and net interest is projected to be roughly three-quarters the size of the budget deficit in 2012. Total revenues are projected to be about half the size of the deficit in 2012. To date, legislation to reduce the budget deficit has focused on reducing discretionary spending, but the budget deficit in 2012 is projected to be more than three quarters the size of total discretionary spending (defense and non-defense combined).

In long-term projections of current policy, unsustainable budget deficits are largely driven by the growth in elderly entitlement spending. By 2050, outlays on Social Security and health programs are projected to exceed total revenues. However, because deficits are already at unsustainable levels today, restraining the future growth rate of elderly entitlement spending alone would still leave an unsustainably large budget deficit—in effect, it would simply keep the deficit from getting larger. Most proposals to curb the future growth of these programs call for gradual changes that exempt those who are now elderly or near-elderly. These types of proposals typically result in modest deficit reduction in the short term.

The Budget Control Act is projected to reduce the deficit by about 1% of GDP on average over the next 10 years, mostly through discretionary spending cuts. If other current policies remain in place, this act would not appear to reduce the deficit enough to restore fiscal sustainability. In this scenario, revenues as a share of GDP will remain below their historical average and mandatory spending will remain at historically high levels as a share of GDP. Revenue levels are currently low because of the recession and tax cuts. The Tax Relief, Unemployment Insurance Reauthorization, and Job Creation Act of 2010 further increased the deficit by an estimated $374 billion in 2011, of which $204 billion is attributable to the extension of expiring tax provisions.

End Notes

[1] All budget data presented in this report are from Congressional Budget Office, Preliminary Analysis of the President's Budget for FY2012, March 2011 and Congressional Budget Office, Budget and Economic Outlook, January 2012 (hereafter referred to as "CBO baseline"), or Office of Management and Budget, FY2013 Budget of the US Government, February 2012 (hereafter referred to as "President's Budget"). The budget deficit is the excess of outlays over revenues in a given year, broadly similar to the amount borrowed from the public that year. The publicly held debt is the accumulation of all past borrowing from the public. The gross debt is the publicly held debt and the intragovernmental debt (the debt that one part of the federal government borrows from another part, mainly government trust funds). All references to years are to fiscal years, unless otherwise noted. For background information on the debt and deficit, see CRS Report WKS0001_Overview, Federal Debt and Deficit: Key Sources, by Justin Murray.

[2] Expressing budget data as a percentage of GDP is most appropriate for making comparisons over extended periods of time because it allows the relative size of those amounts to be consistently compared. Dollar figures are not appropriate because of inflation, which means that a dollar has a smaller amount of purchasing power over time, and because as the economy has become larger, there are more resources available to finance spending through borrowing or taxes.

[3] For information on causes of the budget deficit, see CRS Report R41134, The Impact of Major Legislation on Budget Deficits: 2001 to 2010, by Marc Labonte and Margot L. Crandall-Hollick

[4] Although the FY2011 had already begun, appropriations had not been completed when the January baseline was released.

[5] For more information, see CRS Report R42013, The Budget Control Act of 2011: Effects on Spending Levels and the Budget Deficit, by Marc Labonte and Mindy R. Levit. All of the reductions in spending discussed here would lead to additional declines in spending on net interest because the federal debt would be lower than in the baseline.

[6] For more information, see CRS Report R41965, The Budget Control Act of 2011, by Bill Heniff Jr., Elizabeth Rybicki, and Shannon M. Mahan.

[7] Congressional Budget Office, Testimony Before the Joint Select Committee on Deficit Reduction, US Congress, October 26, 2011. The amount of savings garnered by the Budget

Control Act depends on what baseline it is being compared with. For example, if it were being compared with a baseline based on 2010 levels of discretionary spending, the savings would be higher than if it were compared with 2010 levels.

[8] Congressional Budget Office, Budget and Economic Outlook, January 2012, p. 13.

[9] The Economic Growth and Tax Relief Reconciliation Act of 2001 (EGTRRA; P.L. 107-16) and the Jobs and Growth Tax Relief Reconciliation Act of 2003 (JGTRRA; P.L. 108-27) are popularly referred to as the "Bush tax cuts." Various acts since then have sped up the implementation or prevented the expiration of certain provisions of those acts.

[10] The alternative minimum tax is not adjusted for inflation. As a result, Congress has enacted a series of temporary "patches" to prevent a spike in taxpayers subject to the AMT. See CRS Report RL30149, The Alternative Minimum Tax for Individuals, by Steven Maguire.

[11] Some expiring mandatory spending programs are assumed to continue under the baseline. According to CBO, "The Deficit Control Act specifies some exceptions. For example, spending programs whose authorizations are set to expire are assumed to continue if they have outlays of more than $50 million in the current year and were established at the time of or before the enactment of the Balanced Budget Act of 1997. Programs established after that law was enacted are not automatically assumed to continue but are considered individually in consultation with the budget committees." Congressional Budget Office, Budget and Economic Outlook, January 2012, p. 11. For a list of programs that CBO assumes will expire in its baseline, see Congressional Budget Office, Budget and Economic Outlook, January 2012, Table 3.3.

[12] For more information, see CRS Report R40907, Medicare Physician Payment Updates and the Sustainable Growth Rate (SGR) System, by Jim Hahn and Janemarie Mulvey.

[13] The doc fix is the only expiring mandatory provision that CBO assumes will be continued in its Alternative Fiscal Scenario that is not also included in the current law baseline.

[14] The budgetary effects of extending the AMT patch and Bush tax cuts cannot be separated because of an interactive effect that makes the cost of jointly extending them greater than the cost of extending them separately.

[15] Baseline spending levels for disasters and overseas military operations can be sensitive to the timing of appropriations acts. From the perspective of crafting a deficit reduction proposal, if one believes that a policy included in the baseline is unrealistic, such as a reduction in overseas contingency operations or the omission of future spending in response to an unforeseen emergency in the next 10 years, it can be included in a budget proposal rather than altering the baseline. The adjusted baseline in the President's budget includes a placeholder for future disasters equal to $80 billion over 10 years.

[16] Office of Management and Budget, FY2012 Budget of the US Government, Analytical Perspectives, February 2011, p. 471.

[17] Revenues also rise relative to GDP automatically over time because of "real bracket creep," meaning that the same tax system yields more revenue as national income rises.

[18] In 2008, before ARRA was enacted, non-defense discretionary budget authority was $494 billion. In 2009, it was $803 billion, but in 2011, it was $511 billion.

[19] TARP was created by the Emergency Economic Stabilization Act (P.L. 110-343).

[20] Reductions in TARP's projected lifetime cost led to negative outlays in 2010 and 2011 to compensate for what proved in hindsight to be too large an estimate of its cost in 2009.

[21] Long-term budget data can be found in Congressional Budget Office, The Long-Term Budget Outlook, June 2011. The figures cited here are under CBO's "alternative fiscal scenario." For more information, see CRS Report RL32747, The Economic Implications of the Long-Term Federal Budget Outlook, by Marc Labonte.

[22] In simple terms, saving is measured by the excess of income over spending. When the government's outlays exceed its revenues, it must borrow from the public to finance the difference, and it has a negative saving rate.

[23] Congressional Budget Office, The Budget and Economic Outlook, January 2012, Table C-2.

[24] Economic effects of an unsustainable budget deficit are discussed in CRS Report R40770, The Sustainability of the Federal Budget Deficit: Market Confidence and Economic Effects, by Marc Labonte.

[25] The sustainable deficit is significantly smaller in 2013 than later years because CBO projects low nominal GDP growth in 2013.

[26] Congressional Budget Office, Letter to the Honorable Paul Ryan, February 24, 2011, Table 2.

[27] Congressional Budget Office, The Long-Term Budget Outlook, June 2011, p. 15. Economists call this concept the "fiscal gap."

[28] About half of federal spending on physical capital is for defense, and reduced defense capital spending may not have the same economic effects as reduced non-defense capital spending.

[29] For more information, see CRS Report RL32747, The Economic Implications of the Long-Term Federal Budget Outlook, by Marc Labonte.

[30] This would be the case under the assumptions that discretionary spending and revenues stay around the historical average, as opposed to revenues being determined by current law.

[31] Congressional Budget Office, Long-Term Budget Outlook, June 2011, Figure 3-4.

[32] For a further analysis, see CRS Report R41641, Reducing the Budget Deficit: Tax Policy Options, by Molly F. Sherlock.

[33] For more information, see CRS Report RL33641, Tax Expenditures: Trends and Critiques, by Thomas L. Hungerford.

[34] The reason regular AMT "patches" have been enacted in recent years is to prevent an increase in taxpayers subject to the AMT due to inflation.

In: The Federal Budget: 2013 and Beyond ISBN: 978-1-62081-920-3
Editors: J. Lambert and I. Johnson

Chapter 3

THE BUDGET CONTROL ACT OF 2011: EFFECTS ON SPENDING LEVELS AND THE BUDGET DEFICIT*

Marc Labonte and Mindy R. Levit

SUMMARY

The Budget Control Act of 2011 (BCA) was signed into law by President Obama on August 2, 2011 (P.L. 112-25). In addition to increasing the debt limit, the BCA contained a variety of measures intended to reduce the deficit by at least $2.1 trillion over the FY2012-FY2021 period.

These included $917 billion in savings from statutory caps on discretionary spending and the establishment of a Joint Select Committee on Deficit Reduction.

The BCA discretionary spending caps are projected to result in $917 billion in deficit reduction over the FY2012-FY2021 period. Some types of spending are not subject to the caps, including for spending on Overseas Contingency Operations and emergencies. The precise programmatic impact of these reductions in discretionary spending will be determined in the annual appropriations process. Under the Congressional Budget Office's (CBO's) August 2011 baseline, which

* This is an edited, reformatted and augmented version of a Congressional Research Service publication, CRS Report for Congress R42013, from www.crs.gov, prepared for Members and Committees of Congress, dated November 29, 2011.

incorporates the effects of the BCA, the discretionary spending caps result in a decline in spending in nominal dollar terms in FY2012 and FY2013. Discretionary spending under the caps is projected to decline from 9.0% of GDP in FY2011 to 6.2% of gross domestic product (GDP) in FY2021. Since FY1962, the first year for which data are available, discretionary spending as a percentage of GDP has only been that low in one other year (FY1999).

Beyond the BCA's deficit reduction achieved via the discretionary spending caps, the Joint Committee was created to find additional deficit reduction.

On November 21, 2011, the co-chairs of the Joint Committee announced that they were unable to reach an agreement before the committee's deadline. As a result, a $1.2 trillion automatic spending reduction process has been triggered to begin in January 2013 unless Congress and the President act to eliminate or change the process before then.

The automatic reduction would be divided evenly between defense and non-defense spending. Many large mandatory programs are exempt from this process. The automatic reduction in spending for non-exempt accounts in FY2013 is projected to be 10% for defense, 2% for Medicare, and 7.8% for other mandatory and non-defense discretionary, resulting in further deficit reduction of $1.1 trillion between FY2013 and FY2021. Overall, 85% of the automatic spending cuts in FY2014 are projected to fall on discretionary programs.

Cuts to discretionary spending through the automatic reduction would be in addition to those cuts resulting from the discretionary spending caps. After taking those two provisions into account, total discretionary spending would not regain its 2011 level until 2021 in nominal terms.

While the BCA is projected to reduce the deficit, it does not eliminate budget deficits or growth in the federal debt over the 10-year budget window. Using a current law baseline (where a series of tax cuts are assumed to expire and controls on Medicare payments to doctors are allowed to take effect), budget deficits are estimated to total $3.6 trillion and the federal debt is projected to increase by $4.4 trillion over the next 10 years. Under a current policy baseline (where a series of tax cuts are extended and controls on Medicare payments to doctors are not allowed to take effect), deficits over the next 10 years total $8.6 trillion and the debt would continue to rise faster than GDP. Since the debt cannot perpetually rise faster than GDP, additional spending cuts or revenue increases would eventually be needed.

Since deficit reduction under the BCA is relatively small in FY2012, the short-term effects on the economy should be limited. In the long run, economic theory suggests that large deficits would have negative effects on interest rates, investment spending, trade deficits, and GDP.

INTRODUCTION

Following a lengthy debate over raising the debt limit, the Budget Control Act of 2011 (BCA; P.L. 112-25) was signed into law by President Obama on August 2, 2011.[1] In addition to including a mechanism to increase the debt limit, the BCA contained a variety of measures intended to reduce the deficit, including caps on discretionary spending and an automatic spending reduction process.[2]

According to estimates by the Congressional Budget Office (CBO), the BCA will reduce discretionary spending by $741 billion over the FY2012-FY2021 period, achieved via savings of $756 billion as a result of caps on discretionary spending and $15 billion in increased program integrity spending. Further reductions are achieved in mandatory spending through $16 billion in savings from program integrity initiatives (if the maximum allowable adjustment is subsequently provided) and $5 billion from student loan programs (through higher Pell grant spending and eliminating certain subsidies and incentives for Stafford loans) over 10 years.[3] In addition, all of these changes will lower future debt service costs by $156 billion over 10 years for total spending reductions of $917 billion over the FY2012-FY2021 period.

On November 21, 2011, the co-chairs of the Joint Committee announced that they were unable to reach a deficit-reduction agreement before the committee's deadline. As a result, a $1.2 trillion automatic spending reduction process has been triggered to begin in January 2013 unless Congress and the President enact legislation to eliminate or change the process before then. The automatic reduction ("trigger") would be divided evenly between defense and non-defense spending. The automatic reduction in spending for non-exempt accounts in FY2013 would be 10% for defense, 2% for Medicare, and 7.8% for other mandatory and non-defense discretionary. CBO estimates that this automatic process will reduce outlays by $1.1 trillion over nine years. Together, the discretionary caps and automatic spending reduction process were estimated by CBO to reduce the deficit by $2 trillion over the FY2012-FY2021 period.[4]

The BCA was enacted in response to congressional concern about unsustainable growth in the federal debt and deficit. The federal budget has been in deficit (spending exceeding revenue) since FY2002, but became significantly larger in FY2009. That year, the deficit topped $1 trillion for the first time ever, and it is estimated to remain above $1 trillion in FY2011.[5] Relative to the overall size of the economy, budget deficits from FY2009 to FY2011 have been significantly larger than in any other year since World War

II. From FY1946 to FY2008, budget deficits averaged 1.7% of gross domestic product (GDP) and exceeded 5% of GDP only three times (7.2% in FY1946, 6.0% in FY1983, and 5.1% of GDP in FY1985). From FY2009 to FY2011, budget deficits will average roughly 9.4% of GDP. The federal debt held by the public has grown from 40% of GDP in FY2008 to an estimated 69% of GDP in FY2011. The recent growth in deficits is the result of spending reaching its highest level as a share of GDP since FY1945 and revenues reaching their lowest level as a share of GDP since FY1950. This has occurred largely due to the budgetary effects of the recent recession and policies implemented in response to it.[6]

This report focuses on how the BCA will affect spending and the budget deficit through the "first round" effects, related to discretionary spending caps and student loan provisions, and the "second round" effects of additional deficit reduction, related to the work of the Joint Committee. The report also examines short and long run effects of deficit reduction on the economy. The *Appendix* compares the BCA to past deficit-reduction legislation.

STATUTORY LIMITS ON DISCRETIONARY SPENDING

The BCA sets in statute specific discretionary spending caps on new budget authority between FY2012 and FY2021.[7] Upward revisions to the caps are permitted for purposes of future legislation providing spending designated as "emergency," Overseas Contingency Operations (OCO), program integrity initiatives to curb fraud and abuse in Social Security and federal health programs, and disaster relief.[8] Revisions to the caps for program integrity initiatives are limited to $15 billion over 10 years. Disaster relief funding (defined by the BCA as activities carried out under section 102(2) of the Stafford Act[9]) likewise cannot exceed the average funding provided for disaster relief over the 10 previous fiscal years, excluding the highest and lowest funding years. OMB estimated this figure to be $11.3 billion for the 10 years between FY2002 and FY2011.[10] The levels of emergency and OCO spending are not limited by the BCA.[11] Exempting emergency spending from the caps offers flexibility to future Congresses to respond to unforeseen circumstances, but it also offers a potential avenue for future Congresses to diminish the spending reductions intended by the BCA. Although the BCA allowed for certain policy related adjustments to the caps, the legislation did not allow for any economic adjustments, specifically if inflation turns out to be higher or lower than expected. This means that a higher (lower) than expected rate of inflation would reduce (increase) the purchasing power of discretionary spending permitted under the caps. The BCA did not place similar caps on mandatory spending, which amounted to 56% of total spending in FY2011.

Between FY2012 and FY2013, there are specific caps on new budget authority for the categories of security and non-security spending. For purposes of the discretionary caps, security spending is defined by the BCA as discretionary appropriations associated with agency budgets for the Departments of Defense, Homeland Security, Veterans Affairs, the National Nuclear Security Administration, the intelligence community management account, and all budget accounts in the budget function for international affairs (Function 150).[12] Non-security spending comprises the portion of discretionary spending outside the security category. The largest amounts of spending in the non-security category are tied to the Departments of Health and Human Services, Education, and Housing and Urban Development. In FY2014 and beyond, one cap covers overall discretionary spending.[13]

Outside of the separate caps on security and non-security spending in FY2012 and FY2013, the BCA does not otherwise restrict spending for specific appropriation subcommittees, budget accounts, or functional categories. The Obama Administration stated that the caps would cut approximately $420 billion in security spending over 10 years. Further,

> Assuming roughly proportional cuts, we project that of that $420 billion, $350 billion would be from the budget category of defense, and approximately $330 billion of that would be specifically from the Department of Defense. In sum, this agreement would be consistent with the President's goal for security and Department of Defense savings as laid out in his fiscal framework in April.[14]

However, the BCA does not specify how spending will be allocated across appropriations bills, and which specific programs will be cut to achieve the required savings under the caps, particularly beyond FY2014. This authority is reserved for Congress. If the appropriations process does not result in spending levels that adhere to the cap levels and the cap levels are breached, the BCA stipulates automatic cuts to non-exempt discretionary programs through a sequestration process. Actual total discretionary spending levels over the next 10 years will be determined partly by future Congress's commitment to adhering to the caps and partly by the level at which spending occurs in categories excluded from the caps, such as OCO or emergency spending.[15]

What Happens to Discretionary Spending Under the BCA Relative to Historical Trends?

The BCA was enacted after a period of rapid growth in discretionary spending. (Mandatory spending has also grown and revenue has fallen rapidly relative to GDP in recent years.) Between FY2000 and FY2009, discretionary spending rose by 8.0% per year, on average. Discretionary spending rose by 8.9% in FY2010.[16] Increases in discretionary spending since FY2000 can be attributed primarily to a rise in defense spending throughout the decade, and an increase in spending as a result of economic stimulus programs since 2009.[17] The discretionary funding in the economic stimulus programs was designed such that most discretionary outlays under the act will occur by FY2012. *Table 1* summarizes the discretionary outlay levels in CBO's August 2011 baseline, which incorporate the BCA discretionary spending caps as well as baseline OCO levels and other small adjustments to provide a projection of total discretionary spending.[18] These levels are shown in nominal and real (adjusted for inflation) dollars. Since some categories of discretionary spending are exempt from the caps, total discretionary spending over the next 10 years is unlikely to match the cap levels. Under the August 2011 CBO baseline, discretionary spending in nominal dollars (real dollars) declines by 2.8% (4.0%) in FY2012 and 1.1% (2.4%) in FY2013, but increases (decreases) annually by 1.5% (0.3%), on average, for the rest of the 10-year budget window. Examining levels of discretionary spending going forward may not provide the full picture of changes over time. Between FY2008 and FY2011, total discretionary spending rose from $1,135 billion to $1,353 billion in nominal terms. In nominal terms, total discretionary spending between FY2012 and FY2021 would be above FY2008 levels even if all spending not limited by the caps (such as OCO spending) were zero. Total discretionary spending under the baseline would also be below FY2011 levels until FY2018, in nominal terms. Since FY1962, the first year for which data are available, discretionary spending has fallen in nominal terms only three times, most recently in FY1996. In each case, the previous spending level was surpassed in the following year. If a drawdown of troops occurs as proposed in certain overseas operations, future spending levels will be lower than the baseline levels, absent any other policy changes. Alternatively, if future OCO funding exceeds the levels assumed in the baseline or if there is rapid growth in spending not subject to the caps (such as emergency spending), the overall level of discretionary spending could exceed the level in the baseline over the next 10 years, absent other policy changes.

Table 1. Discretionary Spending Levels and BCA Caps (Outlays)

	2008 Actual	*2011 Actual*	*FY2012*	*FY2013*	*FY2014*	*FY2015*	*FY2016*	*FY2017*	*FY2018*	*FY2019*	*FY2020*	*FY2021*
BCA Spending Caps, Nominal	n/a	n/a	$1,241	$1,170	$1,148	$1,149	$1,164	$1,179	$1,196	$1,226	$1,252	$1,278
$s Billion												
BCA Spending Caps, Real 2011	n/a	n/a	$1,226	$1,141	$1,104	$1,089	$1,085	$1,078	$1,072	$1,078	$1,079	$1,080
$s Billion												
Total Discretionary, Nominal	$1,135	$1,353	$1,315	$1,300	$1,301	$1,311	$1,332	$1,350	$1,370	$1,404	$1,434	$1,464
$s Billiona												
Yr-Yr, Percent Change			-2.8%	-1.1%	0.1%	0.8%	1.6%	1.4%	1.5%	2.5%	2.1%	2.1%
Per Capita ($s)		$4,319	$4,158	$4,071	$4,035	$4,027	$4,053	$4,068	$4,089	$4,152	$4,201	$4,249
Total Discretionary, Real 2011	$1,174	$1,353	$1,299	$1,268	$1,252	$1,243	$1,241	$1,235	$1,228	$1,234	$1,236	$1,237
$s Billiona												
Yr-Yr, Percent Change			-4.0%	-2.4%	-1.3%	-0.7%	-0.2%	-0.5%	-0.6%	0.5%	0.2%	0.1%
Per Capita ($s)		$4,319	$4,107	$3,971	$3,883	$3,818	$3,776	$3,722	$3,666	$3,649	$3,621	$3,590
Total Discretionary,	7.9%	9.0%	8.4%	8.0%	7.7%	7.2%	7.0%	6.7%	6.5%	6.4%	6.3%	6.1%
Percent of GDP[a]												

Source: CRS calculations based on Congressional Budget Office, CBO Analysis of August 1 Budget Control Act, Letter to the Honorable John Boehner and the Honorable Harry Reid, August 1, 2011; Congressional Budget Office, Budget and Economic Outlook: An Update, August 2011; U.S. Census Bureau, Projections of the Population and Components of Change for the United States: 2010 to 2050.

Notes: Spending caps adjusted for inflation using GDP deflator (FY basis). The BCA caps budget authority. This table presents CBO's estimates of outlays based on the BCA cap levels with certain adjustments. Table does not include the effects of the BCA's automatic spending reduction process.

[a]. Levels in the August 2011 CBO Baseline (indicated as "Total Discretionary" in this table) assume the BCA cap level adjusted to include real levels of OCO funding based on current law.

However, a comparison of nominal spending levels over time arguably understates the effects of the discretionary caps on policy for a number of reasons. First, projected inflation over the next 10 years means that a dollar will have less purchasing power in 2021 than it does today. The BCA's nominal discretionary caps do not account for inflation so the declines in spending are larger when converted to real terms (see *Table 1*). If actual inflation turns out to be higher (lower) than projected, real spending cuts will be greater (smaller).

Relative to FY2011, projected spending under the caps in real (inflation-adjusted) terms falls each year until FY2017, and then stays roughly constant. In real terms, total discretionary spending under the baseline, which includes the spending caps and current real levels of OCO, will remain above its FY2008 level but never regain its FY2011 level over the next 10 years.[19] Since FY1997, discretionary spending has only fallen in real terms in one year (FY2007). Since FY1962, there were only two periods where real discretionary spending fell for several years in a row–FY1969- FY1974 and FY1992-FY1996. In the FY1969-FY1974 period, sustained high inflation masked (in real terms) relatively large annual nominal increases. Between FY1992 and FY1996, discretionary spending caps were included as part of the Omnibus Budget and Reconciliation Acts of 1990 and 1993, which contributed to lower overall discretionary spending during that period.

The second reason why the growth in nominal spending levels may understate the effects of the discretionary spending caps is that the population of the United States is projected to rise over the next 10 years. Therefore, the caps will lead to lower discretionary spending per capita than nominal growth rates would indicate for certain functional categories, such as education, training, housing assistance, or health. For these categories, per capita spending would arguably give a better sense of the potential impact of the caps on services than overall spending because it indicates the change in benefits or services available to each individual. However, it remains unknown how any specific program will be impacted by the discretionary spending caps.

As shown in *Table 1*, per capita discretionary spending in nominal terms decreases by 0.2% per year, on average, over the FY2012-FY2021 period. Throughout this period, discretionary spending per capita never regains its FY2011 level and falls from $4,319 in FY2011 to $4,249 in FY2021. After adjusting for inflation and population growth, per capita discretionary spending declines by 1.8% annually, on average, from $4,319 in FY2011 to $3,590 in FY2021.

Finally, the cuts in discretionary spending over the next 10 years would be much larger if discretionary spending is measured as a share of GDP, or relative to the size of the economy. As a percentage of GDP, discretionary spending in FY2008 stood at 7.9%, rising to 9.0% in FY2011.[20] As a percentage of GDP, discretionary spending falls below the FY2008 level in FY2014 and remains below it through FY2021. By FY2021, discretionary spending as a percentage of GDP would be at its lowest level since FY1999.

In the last decade, discretionary spending grew rapidly relative to GDP, taking it back to pre-1990s levels. *Figure 1* illustrates that discretionary spending under the caps is projected to decline from 9.0% of GDP in FY2011 to 6.2% of GDP in FY2021, assuming that OCO outlays (which are not subject to the cap) remain at FY2011 levels in real terms. This would reverse the preceding growth in discretionary spending, taking discretionary spending back down to the historically low levels that prevailed in the late 1990s. Since FY1962, the first year for which data are available, discretionary spending has only been as low as 6.2% of GDP in one other year (FY1999), when OCO spending was nearly zero. If OCO spending declines sufficiently relative to FY2011 levels, at some point during the projection period, discretionary spending would reach its lowest share of GDP ever.

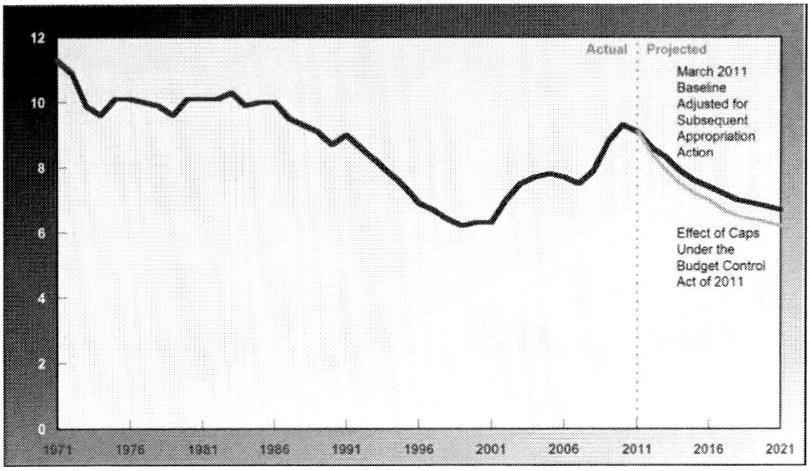

Source: Congressional Budget Office Director's Blog, Discretionary Spending Under the Budget Control Act of 2011, August 8, 2011.

Notes: For illustrative purposes, the figure assumes that discretionary outlays will be equal to the BCA cap amount plus $160 billion to $190 billion each year for overseas contingency operations (which are not subject to the cap).

Figure 1. Discretionary Spending as a Percentage of GDP, 1971-2021.

Most of the decline in discretionary spending as a percentage of GDP was projected to have occurred in the baseline anyway, even in the absence of the BCA caps, due to the baseline assumption that discretionary spending in future years grows at the rate of inflation, which is less than the growth in nominal GDP. Thus, the BCA spending caps represent a reduction in discretionary spending that is in addition to the reductions that result from the assumption that discretionary spending is constant in real terms. That baseline would have already shown a significant drop in discretionary spending relative to its current share of GDP as shown in *Figure 1*. If the baseline were to assume that discretionary spending grew at the same rate as GDP, the reduction in discretionary spending as a result of the BCA caps would be greater than in the CBO score.

In addition to the discretionary caps shown in *Table 1,* discretionary spending would be cut further by the automatic spending reduction process described below.

Comparing Discretionary Savings Relative to Other Measures

Baseline projections of spending, revenue, and the deficit are used as a benchmark to provide an indication of how new legislation, if enacted, would change the projected level relative to current law. For example, when a policy is enacted to cut spending in FY2012, the reduction is measured relative to the baseline projection of spending for FY2012, as opposed to the actual spending level for FY2011. Savings are generally not measured relative to previous year totals since, particularly for mandatory programs and revenue provisions, those levels can change from year to year with no change in law, while discretionary spending is generally subject to the enactment of annual appropriations.[21]

Baselines are used because decisions on the level of discretionary spending are made annually through the appropriations process and it is impossible to know what level of spending will be enacted from one future year to the next. For purposes of the baseline, CBO generally assumes that the level of discretionary spending in future years increases at the rate of inflation.[22] For example, the baseline assumes overseas contingency operations will remain at a constant inflation-adjusted level each year for 10 years. If discretionary spending actually increases at rates above inflation, which it has historically done, then the amount of discretionary spending above inflation is recorded as an increase to discretionary spending relative to the baseline.

Other baselines would be equally valid conceptually, such as ones that freeze discretionary spending in nominal terms or as a percentage of GDP, but are not generally used to score the cost of legislation before Congress.

Compared to the adjusted March 2011 CBO baseline, which accounted for the final FY2011 enacted appropriations bills, the BCA caps make relatively small cuts to discretionary outlays in FY2012. Discretionary spending cuts rise every year thereafter such that the reduction in outlays is nearly five times larger in nominal terms in FY2021, relative to FY2012. However, it is also possible to measure the impact of changes in spending relative to other measures. *Table 2* provides comparisons of the discretionary cap levels to the January 2011 CBO baseline, the FY2012 House Budget Resolution (H.Con.Res. 34), and the President's FY2012 budget request. (For each comparison, OCO outlays and discretionary spending cuts resulting from the trigger are excluded.) The comparison to the January 2011 CBO baseline gives a rough estimate of the combined effects on discretionary spending of the final appropriations for FY2011 and the BCA. For that reason, the spending cuts relative to the January 2011 CBO baseline are somewhat larger than relative to the adjusted March 2011 CBO baseline.

What is a baseline?

Baselines provide a benchmark for comparing how proposed budget policy changes would affect existing policies. The calculation of a baseline can be instrumental to the evaluation of these policies. Conventional scoring procedures would measure a legislative proposal relative to CBO's official baseline, which is a current law baseline. In the current law baseline, CBO assumes that certain policies set to expire under current law will do so as scheduled.

However, changes in policy can also be measured relative to other proposals and baselines. Several of these alternative proposals and their effects are illustrated in Table 2. Other baselines, sometimes referred to as a *current policy* baseline, assume that certain current policies are likely to be extended.

The House Budget Resolution (H.Con.Res. 34) called for lower spending levels than those imposed by the BCA caps each year. Thus, were the levels of spending called for in the House Budget Resolution to be enacted, spending would decline further than it would under the BCA. The larger size of the spending cuts relative to President's budget is partly attributable to the final FY2011 appropriations and to the BCA. The President requested similar levels of discretionary spending, in terms of budget authority (excluding OCO), compared to the January 2011 CBO baseline levels between FY2012 and FY2016, and lower levels between FY2017 and FY2021. The BCA cap levels are lower than the President's request for each year.

THE JOINT SELECT COMMITTEE ON DEFICIT REDUCTION

In addition to the deficit reduction achieved through the statutory caps on discretionary spending discussed above, the BCA calls for the Joint Committee,[23] composed of 12 Members of Congress, to propose legislation that reduces the deficit by at least $1.5 trillion over 10 years, from FY2012-FY2021. If legislation reducing the deficit by at least $1.2 trillion over 10 years is not enacted, an automatic spending reduction process, which is discussed in the next section, goes into effect. There were no restrictions on the types of spending or revenue proposals that the Joint Committee could recommend. On November 21, 2011, the co-chairs of the Joint Committee announced that they were unable to reach an agreement before the committee's deadline. As a result, an automatic spending reduction process has been triggered to begin in January 2013 unless Congress and the President act to eliminate or change the process before then.

Automatic Spending Reduction Process

The BCA set the amount of the automatic spending reduction based on how much deficit reduction resulted from the work of the Joint Committee. Because no deficit reduction legislation was proposed, the amount required from the automatic spending reduction process will be $1.2 trillion. CBO estimates that the deficit reduction achieved by this $1.2 trillion process is $1.1 trillion, for reasons discussed in the next section.

Of the $1.2 trillion in deficit reduction, the BCA specifies that 18% of the total ($216 billion) be credited to debt service savings that would result from the spending reduction.[24] Therefore, the amount of the reduction in budget authority would equal the remaining 82% of the required deficit reduction total.

Table 2. Reductions in Discretionary Spending from the BCA Relative to Selected Alternatives (Outlays in billions of dollars and as a percentage of GDP)

	FY2012	*FY2013*	*FY2014*	*FY2015*	*FY2016*	*FY2017*	*FY2018*	*FY2019*	*FY2020*	*FY2021*
BCA Discretionary Caps Dollar Difference from:	$1,241	$1,170	$1,148	$1,149	$1,164	$1,179	$1,196	$1,226	$1,252	$1,278
CBO January 2011 Baseline	-$33	-$60	-$76	-$84	-$93	-$101	-$110	-$118	-$126	-$134
CBO Adjusted March 2011	-$25	-$47	-$59	-$67	-$74	-$81	-$89	-$97	-$104	-$112
Baseline										
House FY2012 Budget	$73	$56	$53	$60	$71	$81	$91	$99	$107	$110
Resolution										
President's FY2012 Budget[a]	-$73	-$91	-$92	-$89	-$95	-$95	-$98	-$100	-$107	-$101
Percent Difference from:										
CBO January 2011 Baseline	-2.6%	-4.9%	-6.2%	-6.8%	-7.4%	-7.9%	-8.4%	-8.8%	-9.1%	-9.5%
CBO Adjusted March 2011	-2.0%	-3.9%	-4.9%	-5.5%	-6.0%	-6.4%	-6.9%	-7.3%	-7.7%	-8.1%
Baseline										

Table 2. (Continued)

	FY2012	*FY2013*	*FY2014*	*FY2015*	*FY2016*	*FY2017*	*FY2018*	*FY2019*	*FY2020*	*FY2021*
House FY2012 Budget	6.3%	5.0%	4.8%	5.5%	6.5%	7.4%	8.2%	8.8%	9.3%	9.4%
Resolution										
President's FY2012 Budget[a]	-6.6%	-8.0%	-7.9%	-7.6%	-7.9%	-7.8%	-7.8%	-7.8%	-8.1%	-7.6%

Source: CRS calculations based on U.S. Congressional Budget Office, CBO Analysis of August 1 Budget Control Act Letter to the Honorable John Boehner and the Honorable Harry Reid, August 1, 2011, Table 1; U.S. House of Representatives, Budget Committee, Path to Prosperity, Table S-3; Office of Management and Budget, Budget of the U.S. Government FY 2012, February 2011, Table S-11.

Notes: A negative change indicates a decrease from the comparison point (i.e., in FY2012, the CBO January 2011 Baseline level of discretionary spending was $33 billion higher than the FY2012 BCA discretionary cap level). A positive change indicates an increase from the comparison point. All comparisons omit OCO spending.

[a]. The President's Budget only provides a level of discretionary budget authority, not outlays, that excludes OCO. Therefore, the figures in the table showing the level of change in discretionary spending between the BCA discretionary caps and the President's Budget are in terms of terms of budget authority. Table does not include the effects of the BCA's automatic spending reduction process.

The amount of the automatic spending reduction under the BCA is spread evenly over the nine years from FY2013 to FY2021 and applied to defense (defined as budget function 050) and non-defense spending categories and applied proportionally to discretionary and mandatory programs within each of these categories. The automatic spending reduction would amount to a reduction in budget authority of $109.3 billion each year for nine years, with $54.7 billion of the reduction to be applied to defense and $54.7 billion applied to non-defense programs. Within the defense and non-defense categories, some programs are exempted from an automatic spending reduction and the cuts to other programs are limited by statute.[25] For example, an automatic spending reduction to Medicare is limited to 2% of total program spending.[26] While the annual amount of the total automatic spending reduction would not be revised in subsequent years, the amount applied to any given budget account could be recalculated, if the relative size of budget accounts changes or the exempt/non-exempt status of an account changes.

In FY2013, the automatic spending reduction is carried out through an across-the-board sequester (cancellation) of previously authorized budgetary resources. After the first year (FY2013), the automatic spending reduction is carried out through a sequester for mandatory spending and through reductions in the overall discretionary caps, rather than a sequester, for discretionary spending. The sequester is applied proportionately to all non-exempt accounts, while it is left to future Congresses to determine how to apply the reductions to discretionary accounts within the caps. For purposes of the automatic reductions, the BCA creates new discretionary cap levels for defense (defined as budget category 050) and non-defense for the 10-year budget window. The amount of the automatic reduction is then subtracted from the new defense/non-defense cap levels. *Table 3* shows the defense and non-defense cap levels after the $1.2 trillion automatic spending reduction, based on current projections.[27] For purposes of the caps, the distinction between exempt and non-exempt discretionary accounts does not apply. However, certain categories of discretionary spending, such as OCO, would still not apply to the caps. Cuts to discretionary programs as a result of the automatic spending reduction process would be in addition to the cuts resulting from the BCA discretionary caps.

Figure 2 shows the projected percentage of budgetary resources tied to each major programmatic area in FY2014, the first year for which the automatic spending reduction is carried out through revisions to the discretionary caps.[28] Of total gross budgetary resources for FY2014, 51% are mandatory spending that is exempt from the automatic reduction. The other

49% of budgetary resources is subject to the automatic spending reduction process. The mandatory share of nonexempt budgetary resources is subject to a sequester, and the discretionary share is subject to reduction as a result of lower discretionary spending caps. Overall, only $71 billion, or 2%, of budgetary resources in FY2014 are mandatory programs that are subject to a sequester without limits, mostly falling into the non-defense category. The non-exempt portion of Medicare, which also falls into the non-defense category and accounts for 16% of total gross budgetary resources in FY2014, is capped at a maximum reduction of 2% by the BCA. Discretionary spending composes 31% of total budgetary resources in FY2014, 16% in defense and 15% in non-defense.

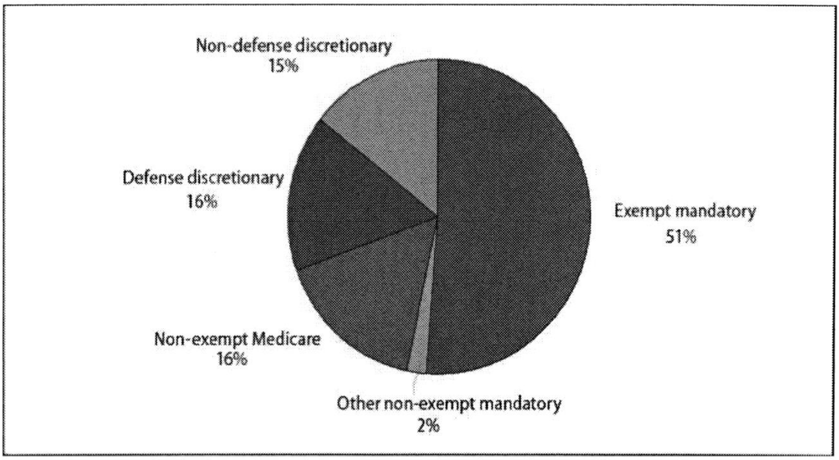

Source: CRS Calculations based on Congressional Budget Office, Estimated Impact of Automatic Budget Enforcement Procedures Specified in the Budget Control Act, September 12, 2011, Table 2.

Note: Categories labeled exempt are not subject to a spending reduction. Other categories are subject to a spending reduction. Does not include OCO spending.

Figure 2. Projected Percentage of Budgetary Resources, by Major Programmatic Area, FY2014.

Figure 3 shows the percentage share of the reduction in FY2014 for each category shown in *Figure 2* under the $1.2 trillion automatic spending reduction process. Most exempt spending is within the non-defense mandatory category, so the automatic spending reductions would fall most heavily, in percentage terms, on discretionary programs. In FY2014, discretionary spending is projected to account for 31% of budgetary resources (see *Figure*

2), but receives 85% of the automatic spending reductions (see *Figure 3*). Defense discretionary spending would be particularly affected because the defense spending category would receive 50% of all automatic cuts (see *Figure 3*) but accounts for 16% of total gross budgetary resources (see *Figure 2*) and 33% of total non-exempt budgetary resources. By contrast, mandatory programs account for 69% of budgetary resources in FY2014, but would bear 15% of the spending reduction (10% on Medicare and 5% on other mandatory programs).

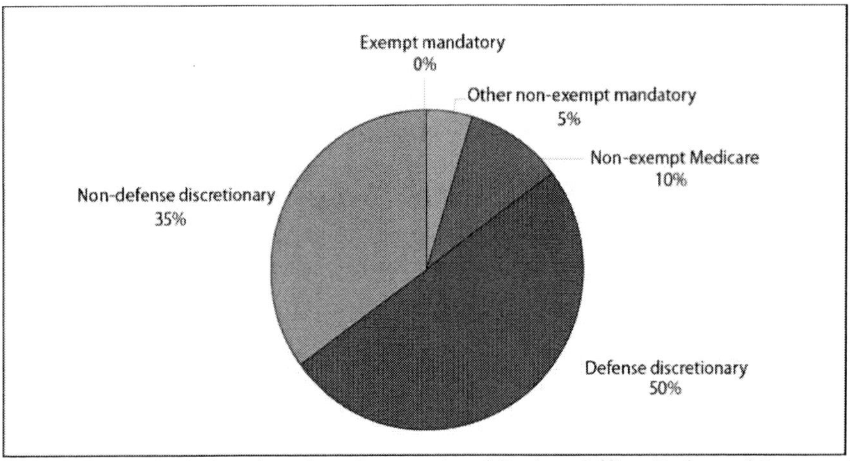

Source: CRS Calculations based on Congressional Budget Office, Estimated Impact of Automatic Budget Enforcement Procedures Specified in the Budget Control Act, September 12, 2011, Table 3.
Note: Does not include OCO spending.

Figure 3. Percentage of Automatic Spending Reduction in Each Major Programmatic Area for a $1.2 Trillion Reduction, FY2014.

Table 3 shows the reductions in spending from FY2013 to FY2021 to different portions of the budget in dollar terms and percentage terms from the $1.2 trillion automatic spending reduction process. Exempting large parts of the budget from an automatic reduction means that the effect on non-exempt programs is much larger than if the same cut were spread over all programs (i.e., there were no exemptions). For example, in *Table 3*, total spending (gross outlays) would be reduced by about 2.5% in FY2014, but it would reduce discretionary caps for defense by 9.8% and non-defense by 7.4% in FY2014. (The percentage cut from the pre-cap baseline would be larger.) It would reduce non-exempt mandatory outlays by 2% for Medicare (because of the

BCA 2% limit) and 7.4% for other non-defense, non-exempt mandatory accounts in FY2014. (The reduction in non-exempt defense mandatory would be less than $1 billion.)[29]

Medicare spending is projected to rise in dollar terms over the next 10 years and therefore, the 2% cut will result in an increase in dollar terms of the amount of the automatic spending reduction being borne by Medicare. Since the total dollar amount of the automatic reduction affecting the non-defense category would be the same each year from FY2013 to FY2021 and the dollar amount borne by Medicare rises, the dollar amount of the reduction that would be borne by the other non-exempt, non-defense programs would fall over the course of the budget window. In the example illustrated by *Table 3*, cuts to Medicare rise from $11 billion in FY2013 to $17 billion in FY2021, while cuts to other non-defense categories fall from $44 billion to $38 billion in those years.

Table 3 also shows the projected discretionary cap amounts for defense and non-defense after the $1.2 trillion automatic spending reduction has been applied. Total discretionary budget authority was $712 billion for defense and $511 billion for non-defense in FY2011. To compare FY2011 levels to projected future levels shown in *Table 3*, some adjustment must be made for activities that are not subject to the cap, namely overseas contingency operations (OCO), emergency spending, and disaster spending. Assuming OCO budget authority were maintained at current levels (adjusted for inflation) and emergency and disaster budget authority were set at zero, defense and non-defense budget authority under the trigger would be below 2011 levels until 2018 in nominal terms. Because of timing differences between budget authority and outlays, total discretionary outlays after the automatic cuts would be below its 2011 level until 2021 in nominal terms.

Table 4 provides a list of some of the largest exempt programs and activities and their FY2010 spending levels, the last year of historical data available for these programs. The programs and activities are classified into defense and non-defense categories. Budget authority for each line item is further classified by type of spending, mandatory or discretionary. For purposes of the automatic spending reduction process, Veterans Programs, for example, are classified as nondefense spending, with $71.2 billion in mandatory budget authority and $53.1 billion in discretionary budget authority in FY2010. Within the defense category, the President has the discretion to exempt or include budget authority for military personnel in the automatic spending reduction process. As previously discussed, the exemptions for discretionary programs are relevant under the sequester in FY2013.

Table 3. $1.2 Trillion Automatic Spending Reduction by Major Category (Budget Authority, FY2013 to FY2021)

	FY2013	FY2014	FY2015	FY2016	FY2017	FY2018	FY2019	FY2020	FY2021
Amount of Reduction in Billions of Dollars									
Defense Reductiona	$55	$55	$55	$55	$55	$55	$55	$55	$55
Non-Defense Reduction	$55	$55	$55	$55	$55	$55	$55	$55	$55
Medicare (Mandatory)	$11	$11	$12	$13	$13	$14	$15	$16	$17
Other Non-Exempt Mandatory	$5	$5	$6	$6	$5	$5	$5	$5	$5
Discretionary	$39	$38	$37	$36	$36	$36	$34	$33	$33
Percentage Reduction									
Defense Reduction	10.0%	9.8%	9.7%	9.5%	9.3%	9.1%	8.9%	8.7%	8.5%
Non-Defense Reduction									
Medicare (Mandatory)	2.0%	2.0%	2.0%	2.0%	2.0%	2.0%	2.0%	2.0%	2.0%
Other Non-Exempt Mandatory	7.8%	7.4%	7.1%	6.8%	6.6%	6.4%	6.1%	5.8%	5.5%
Discretionary	7.8%	7.4%	7.1%	6.8%	6.6%	6.4%	6.1%	5.8%	5.5%
Projected Discretionary Cap									
Levels in Billions of Dollars									
Under $1.2 Trillion Reduction									
Defense	$491	$501	$511	$522	$535	$548	$561	$575	$589
Non-Defense	$462	$472	$483	$494	$505	$517	$532	$545	$557

Source: Congressional Budget Office, Estimated Impact of Automatic Budget Enforcement Procedures Specified in the Budget Control Act, September 12, 2011, Table 3; CRS calculations.

Notes: Totals may not sum due to rounding. Figures are projected; actual amounts for each year will not be determined until that year. a. Mandatory reductions of defense spending account for less than $500 million.

From FY2014 to FY2021, the discretionary changes occur through a reduction in the discretionary caps. For purposes of the caps, the distinction between exempt and non-exempt discretionary accounts does not apply.

Table 4. Selected Programs and Activities Exempt from an Automatic Spending Reduction (FY2010 budget authority in billions of dollars and percentage of category total)

Program or Activity	Mandatory	Discretionary	% of Total Defense(050)	% of Total Non-Defense
Defense (050) Programs:				
Military Personnela		$121.3	16.8%	
Non-Defense Programs:				
Social Security	$701.0			25.4%
Tier I Railroad Retirement Benefits	$6.9			0.3%
Veterans Programs	$71.2	$53.1		4.5%
Refundable Income Tax Credits	$108.9			3.9%
GSE Preferred Stock Purchase Agreementsb	$52.3			1.9%
Federal Retirement and Disability Accountsand Activities	$151.7	$5.7		5.7%
Child Nutrition Programs (with the exception for special milk programs)	$16.9	$0.2		0.6%
Children's Health Insurance Fund	$12.6			0.5%
Family Support Programs	$4.7			0.2%
Grants to States for Medicaid	$292.7			10.6%
Supplemental Nutrition Assistance Program	$69.0	$0.4		2.5%
Supplemental Security Income Program	$47.1	$3.5		1.8%

Program or Activity	Mandatory	Discretionary	% of Total Defense(050)	% of Total Non-Defense
Temporary Assistance to Needy Families	$17.1			0.6%
Federal-Aid Highways[c]	$39.7			1.4%

Source: Office of Management and Budget, Budget of the U.S. Government, Fiscal Year 2012, Budget Appendix, available at http://www.whitehouse.gov/sites/default/files/omb/budget/fy2012/assets/appendix.pdf; Public Budget Database, available at http://www.whitehouse.gov/omb/budget/Supplemental; and Historical Tables, Table 5.1, available at http://www.whitehouse.gov/omb/budget/Historicals/. For a full list of exempt programs and special sequester rules, see 2 USC 905 and 2 USC 906, Section 255 of the Balanced Budget and Emergency Deficit Control Act of 1985, as amended.

Notes: The total percentage of exempt budget authority for all programs and activities would likely exceed the levels shown in this table. Figures in this table are expressed in terms of budget authority because that is what would be automatically reduced if reductions occurred. The table illustrates total spending for each program unless otherwise noted, not necessarily the exempt portion of a program.

[a] Military personnel accounts can be made exempt from an automatic spending reduction only if the President notifies Congress of their exemption before August 10 for the budget year. The accounts can be made entirely exempt or can be reduced by a lower uniform percentage than would otherwise apply.

[b] This figure is in terms of outlays, rather than budget authority because budget authority for this program was not limited by statute.

[c] Funding for Federal-Aid Highways (account 69-8083-0-7-401) is exempt to the extent that the budgetary resources of the program are subject to obligation limitations in the appropriations bill. The figure shown here is the obligation limitation for FY2010 for this account.

The BCA gives the Office of Management and Budget sole authority for allocating the automatic spending reduction across non-exempt accounts under a sequester and calculating the amount of the reduction in the discretionary caps. Were the spending reduction to occur, the cuts to nonexempt account would most likely differ from current estimates because actual program spending levels will change and as a result of both future policy decisions and technical adjustments to projections.

The automatic spending reduction process is not meant to ensure that a certain actual deficit or spending level is attained over time or that deficit saving accomplished by the automatic spending reduction is not undone by future legislation. The amount of automatic spending reduction does not change if future budget deficits turn out to be larger or smaller than projected at the time the automatic spending reduction is determined. Future budget deficits could turn out to be larger or smaller than projected because of subsequent legislative changes or because of forecasting errors, which have historically been large.[30]

Effects of the BCA on the Budget Deficit

CBO estimates that the discretionary caps in the BCA will reduce the baseline deficit by $917 billion over 10 years. The estimated budgetary savings increase from $27 billion in FY2012 to $153 billion in FY2021 (shown in *Table 5*).[31] The effects of the education provisions of the BCA on the deficit are negligible, slightly increasing the deficit in the first three years and then decreasing it for the rest of the projection.

CBO estimated that the automatic spending reduction process would reduce the deficit by $1.1 trillion over nine years, rather than the $1.2 trillion called for in the BCA. The distribution of deficit reduction over the nine years would rise from $68 billion in 2013 to $148 billion in 2021. The difference in amount and timing from what is called for in the BCA is due to three issues. First, the automatic spending reduction process reduces budget authority, but the deficit is influenced by outlays. A change in budget authority leads to a gradual change in outlays because of the time lag between when spending is authorized and when it occurs. As a result, CBO projects some reduction in outlays after 2021. Second, CBO projects that the interest savings would be less than the $216 billion (18% of $1.2 trillion) assumed in the BCA. Third, "reductions in budgetary resources for some programs and activities ... would have effects that would offset some of the original savings..."[32]

Is the deficit reduction achieved by the BCA insufficient, requiring additional policy changes in the future to further reduce the deficit? Or does it reduce deficits excessively? It depends on the policy goal. A goal of the deficit reduction provisions of the BCA was to match the BCA's multistep increase in the debt limit, although the savings is over a different timeframe than the debt limit increase and the deficit reduction achieved in the BCA in isolation would not prevent the need for future debt limit increases. In any case, matching deficit reduction with debt limit increases is a intermediate goal, but not an ultimate goal of fiscal policy.

Table 5. Budget Deficit Projections With and Without the BCA

	FY2012	FY2013	FY2014	FY2015	FY2016	FY2017	FY2018	FY2019	FY2020	FY2021	FY2012-FY2021
				Billions of $							
Baseline Deficit Prior to the Enactment of the BCA (Current Law)	$997	$667	$441	$399	$489	$462	$462	$529	$570	$596	$5,615
Effects of Discretionary Caps on Deficit	-$27	-$50	-$64	-$74	-$85	-$97	-$110	-$122	-$137	-$153	-$917
Effects of Education Provisions on Deficit	+$3	+$6	+$3	-$2	-$2	-$2	-$2	-$2	-$2	-$3	-$5
Effects of Automatic Spending Reduction on Deficit	$0	-$68	-$94	-$105	-$114	-$122	-$129	-$135	-$142	-$148	-$1,057
Baseline Deficit Including BCA (Current	$973	$555	$286	$218	$288	$241	$221	$270	$289	$292	$3,634
Law)											
Deficit Including BCA (Current Policy)	$996	$815	$658	$647	$773	$787	$832	$949	$1,044	$1,129	$8,630
				% of GDP							
Baseline Deficit Prior to the Enactment of the BCA (Current Law)	6.4%	4.1%	2.6%	2.2%	2.6%	2.3%	2.2%	2.4%	2.5%	2.5%	n/a
Effects of Discretionary Caps on Deficit	-0.2%	-0.3%	-0.4%	-0.4%	-0.4%	-0.5%	-0.5%	-0.6%	-0.6%	-0.6%	n/a
Effects of Education Provisions on Deficit	*	*	*	*	*	*	*	*	*	*	n/a
Effects of Automatic Spending Reduction on Deficit	0%	-0.4%	-0.6%	-0.6%	-0.6%	-0.6%	-0.6%	-0.6%	-0.6%	-0.6%	n/a
Baseline Deficit Including BCA (Current Law)	6.2%	3.4%	1.7%	1.2%	1.5%	1.2%	1.1%	1.2%	1.3%	1.2%	n/a

Table 5. (Continued)

	FY2012	FY2013	FY2014	FY2015	FY2016	FY2017	FY2018	FY2019	FY2020	FY2021	FY2012-FY2021
				Billions of $							
Deficit Including BCA (Current Policy)	6.4%	5.0%	3.9%	3.6%	4.1%	3.9%	4.0%	4.3%	4.6%	4.7%	n/a

Source: CRS calculations based on CBO data.

Notes: Includes effects of lower debt service. Negative numbers reduce deficit, positive numbers increase deficit. Columns may not sum due to rounding. Deficit effect of caps is calculated here using CBO's August baseline; the original score was calculated using CBO's adjusted March baseline and was $890 billion over 10 years. * = <0.1% of GDP. See Table 6 for bridge from Current Law Baseline to Current Policy Baseline.

Table 6. Current Law and Current Policy Baseline Projections (billions of dollars)

	FY2012	*FY2013*	*FY2014*	*FY2015*	*FY2016*	*FY2017*	*FY2018*	*FY2019*	*FY2020*	*FY2021*	*FY2012-FY2021*
Current Law Baselinea	$973	$555	$286	$218	$288	$241	$221	$270	$289	$292	$3,634
+ Extend Tax Cuts and Index	$11	$241	$348	$402	$453	$510	$570	$633	$702	$778	$4,648
AMT to Inflation											
+ Extend Doc Fix	$12	$19	$24	$27	$32	$36	$41	$46	$53	$59	$349
= Current Policy Baseline	$996	$815	$658	$647	$773	$787	$832	$949	$1,044	$1,129	$8,630

Source: CRS calculations based on Congressional Budget Office, The Budget and Economic Outlook: An Update, August 2011, Tables 1-1 and 1-8.

Note: AMT = alternative minimum tax

[a]. Includes the effects of the deficit reduction provisions of the Budget Control Act.

Two other potential goals of deficit reduction could be to balance the budget or place the deficit on a sustainable path. In order to evaluate whether the BCA accomplishes either goal, it is first necessary to discuss the range of projections of future deficits.

Projections of future deficits depend on underlying assumptions, particularly the treatment of expiring provisions. In the "current law" baseline, certain policies set to expire under current law will do so as scheduled.[33] For example, the baseline assumes that expiring tax provisions, such as the 2001/2003/2010 ("Bush") tax cuts that are set to expire at the end of calendar year 2012, will expire as scheduled. Other provisions, such as the indexing of the alternative minimum tax (AMT) to inflation and the "doc fix" that Congress has enacted annually to prevent significant cuts to Medicare physician payments, are also assumed to expire as scheduled.[34] Baseline deficits could potentially be projected under several other alternative assumptions. For example, *Table 6* illustrates how the extensions of "current policy" would change the deficit outlook relative to the current law baseline, by assuming that the tax cuts are extended, the AMT is indexed to inflation, and the doc fix is enacted. Under these assumptions, the budget deficit would be $5 trillion greater over the FY2012-FY2021 period than under the current law baseline.[35]

While the BCA is not projected to result in a balanced budget, another policy goal may be to place the deficit on a sustainable path, meaning a level that would stabilize the debt as a share of GDP. Economists believe that the budget will eventually need to be placed on a sustainable path since debt service cannot rise faster than income indefinitely.[36] Whether or not the BCA's forecast accomplishes this depends on what assumptions are used in the baseline.

Under the current policy baseline that incorporates the effects of the BCA, deficits are projected to be $8.5 trillion—$5 trillion larger than the current law deficits—over 10 years. Under the current policy baseline, deficits never get lower than 3.9% of GDP (rising to 4.7% of GDP by FY2021) and the debt continues to rise relative to GDP each year, reaching 82% of GDP by FY2021.[37] If one believes that current policies will be maintained, additional policy changes beyond the BCA would be required to put the deficit on a sustainable path.

Under current law, budget deficits fall to 1% of GDP in FY2018 (rising slightly thereafter) and the publicly held debt falls as a share of GDP over the next 10 years—although it will still remain at levels that are historically high for the post-World War II period—placing policy back on a sustainable path.

In other words, allowing the "Bush tax cuts," AMT "patch," and "doc fix" to Medicare to expire would be one set of policy changes that would place the deficit on a sustainable basis. CRS cannot recommend whether these policy options are more or less desirable than various alternatives. (Indeed, even without the BCA, budget deficits were projected to have become low enough under current law to temporarily stabilize the debt relative to GDP.) Beyond the 10-year budget window, unsustainably large budget deficits are projected to reappear, primarily driven by the assumption that health care costs will continue to grow faster than GDP.[38]

EFFECTS OF THE BCA ON THE ECONOMY

Gross domestic product, the total output of the economy, consists of spending on consumption, investment, net exports, and by government. In the short run, policy changes that reduce the budget deficit by reducing government spending would directly reduce that component of gross domestic product.[39] As a result, in an economy that is significantly below full employment (as is the case today), standard macroeconomic theory predicts that reducing the deficit would reduce spending and employment in the overall economy, all else equal. To fully offset these effects, other spending in the economy would need to rise. Yet in an economy where overall spending is already too low to fully employ all available labor and capital resources, other spending is unlikely to increase sufficiently.[40] Theory predicts that, in an open economy, the short-term effects of changes in the budget deficit on overall spending in the economy would be diminished by cross-border capital flows.[41] Theory also predicts that these effects would be temporary– eventually, market forces would return the economy to full employment. This would happen more slowly if the budget deficit were reduced, compared to if the budget deficit were maintained.[42] CBO is projecting that the economy will be back to full employment around 2016.

This analysis assumes that investors will continue to be willing to finance large budget deficits at low interest rates in the short term regardless of whether the budget deficit is reduced. If the United States entered a "debt spiral," the standard macroeconomic analysis may no longer apply. A "debt spiral" is a scenario similar to that recently experienced in Greece, where investors lose faith in the government's ability to service its debt, and therefore require much higher interest rates to be willing to hold government debt. In this scenario, policy changes to reduce the budget deficit could potentially stimulate the economy, if it restored investor confidence and, as a result, interest rates declined. There is no evidence that the United States is about to enter a debt spiral at this time, and most economists consider the likelihood of a debt spiral to be small. While investors may be willing to finance large budget deficits at low interest rates for several more years, the risk of a crisis remains for as long as the United States continues to run unsustainably large budget deficits.[43]

Reducing the budget deficit through spending cuts would also be expected to affect the economy in the long run. In standard macroeconomic theory, budget deficits "crowd out" private investment spending on plant and equipment by pushing up interest rates. In other words, the government's borrowing places upward pressure on all interest rates, leading private businesses to undertake fewer investment projects. Lower investment spending would reduce long run GDP relative to if the budget were balanced, all else equal. Alternatively, standard theory predicts that higher interest rates could be avoided if the government or private sector increases its borrowing from abroad. By accounting identity, this borrowing from abroad comes to the United States in the form of a trade deficit.[44] Chronically low domestic savings rates and chronically high trade deficits in the past two decades suggest that the crowding out problem could become an issue once investment demand rebounds from the economic downturn, if large deficits remain. Reducing budget deficits would reverse such crowding out effects.[45] In addition to the deficit channel, reductions in spending could have positive or negative effects on long-term growth, depending on what type of spending is cut. For example, reducing public investment spending could have negative effects on long-term growth.

The magnitudes of both the short-run and long-run effects described in this section depend mostly on the size of the deficit reduction. Relatively small spending reductions would be expected to have a relatively small effect on the economy, and larger ones would have a larger effect. The magnitude of the short-run effects would also depend on timing. For example, if spending cuts were enacted today but did not go into effect until future years, they would not be expected to have any effect on the economy this year.[46] If the economy were closer to full employment by the time a phased-in spending reduction went into effect, the effects on overall spending in the economy would be expected to be smaller. Eventually, the budget deficit can be restored to sustainability only through spending cuts, tax increases, or both. In that sense, a comparison between reducing the deficit and the status quo is a false comparison in the long run. The size of current deficits should make crowding out effects greater than they have been historically; the weakness in the economy and financial system should make them smaller than historically for the time being.

For determining the short-run macroeconomic effects, thc magnitude of the incremental change in the structural deficit each year is a relevant measure. As seen in *Table 5*, the "first round" cuts relative to the baseline caused by the discretionary spending caps and student loan provisions reduce the deficit by $24 billion in FY2012. They rise around $20 billion each year after that, reaching $156 billion by FY2021. A spending cut of $24 billion amounts to about two-tenths of one percent of GDP in FY2012. Thus, the first round cuts would be expected to be too small to have a noticeable effect on the economy. JPMorgan Chase estimates that the first round cuts would reduce GDP growth by 0.14 percentage points in FY2012[47]–this is relatively small compared to the expected rate of GDP growth that year. On the other hand, GDP growth was already expected to be too slow to significantly reduce the high rate of unemployment in FY2012. Further, some economists fear that the U.S. may be heading back into a recession. If so, deficit reduction in FY2012 could make a recession more likely.[48] Including the automatic spending reduction, spending would be cut by 0.6% of GDP each year (in addition to the first round cuts), beginning in 2013. The two rounds combined amount to about 1% of GDP each year.

The deficit-reduction effects of the Budget Control Act are occurring at the same time that other temporary fiscal stimulus measures are being withdrawn. Thus, the overall stance of current fiscal policy is more contractionary than the BCA viewed in isolation. CBO estimates the combined effects of the BCA and the expiration of the tax cuts (assuming Congress did not extend them) would reduce real GDP by 1.5%-3.5% from what it otherwise would be in FY2013.[49] J.P. Morgan Chase estimates that the structural deficit (adjusting for the business cycle) will decline by 2.3% of GDP in FY2012 overall, and this will reduce GDP growth by 1.7 percentage points, all else equal. In other words, even before the BCA was enacted, the tightening of fiscal policy would have reduced GDP growth by 1.4 percentage points of GDP in FY2012.[50] Similarly, Goldman Sachs estimates that fiscal policy will contract by 1.7% of GDP overall in FY2012, mostly because of expiring provisions.[51]

For determining the long-run macroeconomic effects, the magnitude of the overall decline in the deficit is a relevant measure. As seen in *Table 5*, the BCA reduces deficits by about 1% of GDP from 2013 on. This would reduce the crowding out effects, but leave unsustainably large deficits in place using a current policy baseline. Including the automatic spending reduction, the deficit would still be above a sustainable level under a current policy baseline. Thus, the Budget Control Act would be expected to reduce the long-term crowding out problem, but under a current policy baseline the problem would still be significant, and some risk of a debt spiral would remain. By contrast, under a current law baseline, crowding out would remain, but it would be smaller, and the deficit would be sustainable over 10 years (although large deficits would eventually be projected to reappear in the long run), further reducing the risk of a debt spiral.

APPENDIX. THE RELATIVE SIZE OF THE DEFICIT REDUCTION IN THE BUDGET CONTROL ACT COMPARED TO EARLIER ACTS

The BCA is not the first piece of legislation enacted with the main purpose of reducing the budget deficit. Since the early 1980s, there have been seven major deficit reduction packages which are summarized below.

The Omnibus Budget and Reconciliation Act of 1981 (OBRA 1981; P.L. 97-35) contained major spending changes to certain programmatic areas such as health program block grants, Medicaid, television and radio licenses, Food Stamps, dairy price supports, energy assistance, education program block grants, student loans, the Social Security minimum benefit, and others. It was projected to reduce the deficit by $131 billion over three years.

The Tax Equity and Fiscal Responsibility Act of 1982 (TEFRA 1982; P.L. 97-248) had various provisions that on net increased tax revenue and reduced entitlement spending. It was projected to reduce the deficit by $116 billion over three years.

The Deficit Reduction Act of 1984 (DRA 1984; P.L. 98-369) had various provisions that, on net, increased tax revenue and reduced outlays. It was projected to reduce the deficit by $125 billion over five years.

The Omnibus Budget and Reconciliation Act of 1987 (OBRA 1987; P.L. 100-203) contained major changes to spending and revenue programs. Major spending changes affected such areas as Medicare, Medicaid, agricultural target prices, farm income support payments, deferral of lump-sum retirement payments to federal employees, Postal Service payments into retirement and health benefit funds, and others. Major revenue changes affected such areas as home mortgage interest deduction, deduction of mutual fund expenses, accelerated payments of corporate estimated taxes, and others. It was projected to reduce the deficit by $76 billion over two years.

The Omnibus Budget and Reconciliation Act of 1990 (OBRA 1990, P.L. 101-508) had various provisions that on net increased tax revenue and reduced mandatory spending. In addition, it set discretionary spending targets below baseline levels for future years with enforcement mechanisms to ensure the targets were met. It was projected to reduce the deficit by $423 billion over five years. The Omnibus Budget and Reconciliation Act of 1993 (OBRA 1993, P.L. 103-66) had various provisions that on net increased tax revenue and reduced mandatory spending. In addition, it set discretionary spending targets for 1996-1998 below baseline levels for future years, using the same enforcement mechanisms put in place in 1990. It was projected to reduce the deficit by $386 billion over five years.

The Balanced Budget Act of 1997 (BBA 1997; P.L. 105-33) had various provisions that, on net, reduced mandatory spending and reduced the deficit through asset sales. The legislation also contained caps on discretionary spending through FY2002. The BBA was projected to reduce the deficit by $217 billion over five years. The Deficit Reduction Act of 2005 (DRA 2005; P.L. 109-171) had various provisions that on net reduced mandatory spending and was projected to reduce the deficit by $39 billion over five years.

Table A-1 and Table A-2 compare the amount of projected deficit reduction relative to the baseline achieved by various legislation enacted since the 1980s. Over five years, the Budget Control Act of 2011 is projected to be larger in nominal dollars than any other deficit reduction package since 1980. It is smaller than all but two (the Deficit Reduction Act of 1984 and the Deficit Reduction Act of 2005) in the first year, however, due to the fact that the automatic spending reductions are not scheduled to occur until year two. Most of the reason it is larger than previous deficit reduction packages is because the economy is larger. As a percent of GDP, it is smaller than the 1981, 1982, 1990, and 1993 packages.

Table A-1 provides estimates of the deficit effects of this legislation relative to the baseline, in isolation of other legislation enacted in the same year that increased or decreased the deficit. (*Table A-2* shows the effects of the deficit reduction legislation in terms of GDP.) Whether the actual deficit rose or fell compared to the previous year following the enactment of this legislation depends on the other legislation enacted at the time, as well as factors outside of congressional control, such as economic conditions or increases in mandatory spending as a result of demographic changes.

Table A-1. Effects on Budget Deficit of Selected Legislation in Billions of Dollars

	Year 1	*Year 2*	*Year 3*	*Year 4*	*Year 5*	*5 Year Total*	*Deficit in Year of Enactment*
OBRA 1981	$35	$44	$51	n/a	n/a	n/a	$79
TEFRA 1982	$25	$40	$51	n/a	n/a	n/a	$128
DRA 1984	$15	$21	$28	$29	$32	$125	$185
OBRA 1987	$30	$46	n/a	n/a	n/a	n/a	$150
OBRA 1990	$32	$65	$79	$114	$133	$423	$221
OBRA 1993	$32	$53	$75	$104	$122	$386	$255
BBA 1997	-$11	$14	$49	$50	$115	$217	$22
DRA 2005	$5	-$4	$5	$21	$12	$39	$318
BCA 2011	$22	$108	$148	$169	$181	$628	$1,299

Source: CRS Report RS22098, Deficit Impact of Reconciliation Legislation Enacted in 1990, 1993, 1997, and 2006; CRS Report R40480, Budget Reconciliation Measures Enacted Into Law: 1980-2010, by Megan Suzanne Lynch; Congressional Budget Office, Effects of Changes in Taxes and Benefit Payments Resulting from the Tax Equity and Fiscal Responsibility Act of 1982, Staff Memorandum, July 1982; Congressional Budget Office, Budget and Economic Outlook: An Update, Congressional Budget Office, Budgetary Implications of the Balanced Budget Act of 1997, Staff Memorandum, Dec. 1997; Congressional Budget Office, S. 1932 Deficit Reduction Act of 2005, Cost Estimate, January 27, 2006.

Notes: Table does not include effects of debt service savings on the budget deficit. Positive numbers indicate an decrease in the deficit. Negative numbers indicate a increase in the deficit. Deficit reduction estimates are projected at time of enactment.

Table A-2. Effects on Budget Deficit of Selected Legislation as a Percentage of GDP

	Year 1	Year 2	Year 3	Year 4	Year 5	5 Year Average	Deficit in Year of Enactment
OBRA 1981	1.1%	1.3%	1.3%	n/a	n/a	n/a	2.6%
TEFRA 1982	0.7%	1.0%	1.2%	n/a	n/a	n/a	4.0%
DRA 1984	0.4%	0.5%	0.6%	0.6%	0.6%	0.5%	4.8%
OBRA 1987	0.4%	0.6%	n/a	n/a	n/a	n/a	3.2%

Table A-2. (Continued)

	Year 1	Year 2	Year 3	Year 4	Year 5	5 Year Average	Deficit in Year of Enactment
OBRA 1990	0.5%	1.0%	1.2%	1.6%	1.8%	1.3%	3.9%
OBRA 1993	0.5%	0.7%	1.0%	1.3%	1.4%	1.0%	3.9%
BBA 1997	-0.1%	0.2%	0.5%	0.5%	1.1%	0.4%	0.3%
DRA 2005	*	*	*	0.2%	0.1%	0.1%	2.6%
BCA 2011	0.2%	0.7%	1.0%	1.1%	1.1%	0.8%	8.7%

Source: CRS Report RS22098, Deficit Impact of Reconciliation Legislation Enacted in 1990, 1993, 1997, and 2006; Congressional Budget Office, Effects of Changes in Taxes and Benefit Payments Resulting from the Tax Equity and Fiscal Responsibility Act of 1982, Staff Memorandum, July 1982; Congressional Budget Office, Budget and Economic Outlook: An Update, Congressional Budget Office, Budgetary Implications of the Balanced Budget Act of 1997, Staff Memorandum, Dec. 1997; Congressional Budget Office, S. 1932 Deficit Reduction Act of 2005, Cost Estimate, January 27, 2006.

Notes: Table does not include effects of debt service savings on the budget deficit. Positive numbers indicate an decrease in the deficit. Negative numbers indicate a increase in the deficit. Deficit reduction estimates are projected at time of enactment. * = < 0.1%

End Notes

[1] For an overview of changes to the debt limit in the Budget Control Act, see CRS Report RL31967, The Debt Limit: History and Recent Increases, by D. Andrew Austin and Mindy R. Levit.

[2] For an overview of the Budget Control Act, see CRS Report R41965, The Budget Control Act of 2011, by Bill Heniff Jr., Elizabeth Rybicki, and Shannon M. Mahan.

[3] Student loan provisions of the BCA are analyzed in CRS Report R41965, The Budget Control Act of 2011, by Bill Heniff Jr., Elizabeth Rybicki, and Shannon M. Mahan. For more information on student loan programs, see CRS Report R40122, Federal Student Loans Made Under the Federal Family Education Loan Program and the William D. Ford Federal Direct Loan Program: Terms and Conditions for Borrowers, by David P. Smole and CRS Report R41437, Federal Pell Grant Program of the Higher Education Act: Background, Recent Changes, and Current Legislative Issues, by Shannon M. Mahan.

[4] These savings are measured relative to the March 2011 Adjusted Baseline as detailed in CBO Analysis of August 1 Budget Control Act Letter to the Honorable John Boehner and the Honorable Harry Reid, August 1, 2011, Table 3, available at http://www.cbo.gov/ftpdocs/123xx/doc12357/BudgetControlActAug1.pdf in Congressional Budget Office, Estimated Impact of Automatic Budget Enforcement Procedures Specified in the Budget Control Act, September 12, 2011. For details on the effects of specific provisions of the BCA on the deficit, see Table 5.

[5] All budget data presented in this report are from Congressional Budget Office, The Budget and Economic Outlook: An Update, August 2011 (hereinafter referred to as "CBO baseline"), Preliminary Analysis of the President's Budget for FY2012, March 2011 and The Budget and Economic Outlook: Fiscal Years 2011 to 2021, January 2011, or Office of Management and Budget, FY2012 Budget of the U.S. Government, February 2011. The budget deficit is the excess of outlays over revenues in a given year, broadly similar to the amount borrowed from the public that year. The debt held by the public is the accumulation of all past borrowing from the public. The gross debt is the debt held by the public and the intragovernmental debt (the debt that one part of the federal government owes to another part of the government, mainly government trust funds). For background information on the debt and deficit, see CRS Report WKS0001_Overview, Federal Debt and Deficit: Key Sources, by Justin Murray.

[6] For an overview of causes of large deficits and policy options to reduce them, see CRS Report R41778, Reducing the Budget Deficit: Policy Issues, by Marc Labonte and CRS Report R41685, The Federal Budget: Issues for FY2011, FY2012, and Beyond, by Mindy R. Levit.

[7] Appropriations acts provide new budget authority. The budget deficit represents the level of spending, as measured by outlays, in excess of revenues. The outlays for a fiscal year result from the budget authority provided in that fiscal year as well as some budget authority provided in previous fiscal years. Included in the outlay level are all types of spending (i.e., emergency, non-emergency, overseas contingency operations) occurring during the fiscal year.

[8] Revisions are also permitted to be made once a year by the Office of Management and Budget (OMB), which can adjust the discretionary caps to reflect changes in budget concepts and definitions in consultation with the Committees on Appropriations and Budget.

[9] For more information, see CRS Report RL33053, Federal Stafford Act Disaster Assistance: Presidential Declarations, Eligible Activities, and Funding, by Francis X. McCarthy.

[10] Office of Management and Budget, OMB Report on Disaster Relief Funding to the Committees on Appropriations and the Budget of the U.S. House of Representatives and the Senate, September 1, 2011, available at http://www.whitehouse.gov/sites/default/files/omb/assets/legislative_reports/disaster_relief_report_sept2011.pdf

[11] Section 101 of the BCA defines emergency spending to be spending that "the Congress designates as emergency requirements in statute on an account by account basis and the President subsequently so designates." Section 101 of the BCA also defines Overseas Contingency Operations as spending that "the Congress designates for Overseas Contingency Operations/Global War on Terrorism in statute on an account by account basis and the President subsequently so designates."

[12] The security/non-security division of discretionary spending was first used by President George W. Bush and was continued under the Obama Administration. However, the Obama Administration changed the definition of security spending. The definition used by the Obama mirrors the definition used in the BCA, though it does not include the intelligence community management account, which totaled approximately $700 million in discretionary budget authority FY2010. CBO has not regularly reported discretionary spending in terms of security and non-security spending. For more information, see CRS Report RL34424, Trends in Discretionary Spending, by D. Andrew Austin and Mindy R. Levit.

[13] Upward revisions to the discretionary spending caps in FY2014 and beyond are also permitted as discussed above. As a result of the Joint Committee being unable to reach an agreement, the BCA specifies that the automatic spending reduction process categorize spending into

defense and non-defense groupings from FY2013 onward, rather than the security/non-security split discussed here.

[14] U.S. Office of Management and Budget, Security Spending in the Deficit Agreement, OMBlog, August 4, 2011, available at http://www.whitehouse.gov/ blog/2011/08/04/security-spending-deficit-agreement.

[15] Emergency spending received a similar exemption from discretionary spending caps in earlier deficit reduction legislation, and after remaining relatively low in the first eight years that this legislation was in effect, emergency budget authority averaged $38.5 billion per year from 1999 to 2002. U.S. Congressional Budget Office, The Budget and Economic Outlook: Fiscal Years 2003 to 2013, January 2003, Table A-2.

[16] U.S. Congressional Budget Office, The Budget and Economic Outlook: An Update, August 2011, p. 17.

[17] For more information, see CRS Report RL34424, Trends in Discretionary Spending, by D. Andrew Austin and Mindy R. Levit.

[18] Because the level of OCO funding was not specified in the BCA, the current CBO baseline maintains OCO funding at FY2011 levels in inflation-adjusted terms. As a result, current baseline levels are likely to differ from actual spending levels since OCO spending is not anticipated to remain equal to FY2011 real levels for the next 10 years. The August 2011 baseline does not include spending permitted under the BCA on disasters, emergency, or program integrity initiatives. Although the BCA caps budget authority rather than outlays, this report generally discusses the change in discretionary outlays over the next decade as outlay levels are used to calculate the budget deficit and reflect what is actually spent in a given year.

[19] If spending outside the caps, notably OCO spending, were very low, then total discretionary spending in real terms would remain below FY2008 levels for the next 10 years.

[20] Discretionary spending as a percentage of GDP peaked in FY2010 at 9.3%.

[21] For more information regarding baselines and how they are constructed, see CRS Report 98-560, Baselines and Scorekeeping in the Federal Budget Process, by Bill Heniff Jr. and CRS Report R41778, Reducing the Budget Deficit: Policy Issues, by Marc Labonte.

[22] As a result of the BCA, the new baseline discretionary spending levels are set as the discretionary spending caps created in the legislation, with modifications made for exempt categories such as overseas contingency operations. Going forward, the costs of future policy proposals will be evaluated against this new baseline. Prior to the enactment of the BCA, CBO utilized the baseline rules contained in Section 257 of the Balanced Budget and Emergency Deficit Control Act of 1985, as amended (Title II of P.L. 99-177).

[23] The Committee's website can be accessed at http://deficitreduction.senate.gov/public/.

[24] The actual amount of debt service savings will depend on future interest rates and the timing of the deficit reduction; 18% was set by the BCA. As described in CBO's analysis of the net budgetary savings resulting from an automatic $1.2 trillion reduction in the event a Joint Committee bill is not enacted, debt service savings amount to 16% of the total between FY2013 and FY2021. See Congressional Budget Office, Estimated Impact of Automatic Budget Enforcement Procedures Specified in the Budget Control Act, September 12, 2011.

[25] These exemptions and special sequester rules are found in 2 USC 905 and 2 USC 906, Section 255 and 256 of the Balanced Budget and Emergency Deficit Control Act of 1985, as amended.

[26] Some Medicare spending is exempt from automatic spending reductions, including Medicare Part D low-income and catastrophic subsidies and qualified individual (QI) premiums. For more information see 2 USC 906(d)(7).

[27] For non-defense discretionary, actual cap amounts for each year will not be determined until that year.

[28] OCO is excluded from Figure 2 and Figure 3. If it were included at 2011 levels, defense discretionary would rise to 20% of total budgetary resources and overall mandatory spending would decline to 66% of total budgetary resources (see Figure 2).

[29] Data from CBO referenced in this section can be found in Congressional Budget Office, Estimated Impact of Automatic Budget Enforcement Procedures Specified in the Budget Control Act, September 12, 2011. Two other estimates of the cuts under a $1.2 trillion automatic spending reduction by non-governmental organizations can be found at Bipartisan Policy Center, How the Sequester Works if the Joint Select Committee Fails, August 5, 2011, available at http://www.bipartisanpolicy.org/blog/2011/08/how-sequester-works-if-joint-select-committee-fails; Center on Budget and Policy Priorities, How the Potential Across-the-Board Cuts in the Debt Limit Deal Would Occur, August 8, 2011, available at http://www.cbpp.org/cms/index.cfm?fa=view&id=3557.

[30] For more information on the accuracy of projections, see Congressional Budget Office, CBO's Economic Forecasting Record: 2010 Update, July 2010, available at http://www.cbo.gov/ftpdocs/115xx/doc11553/ ForecastingAccuracy.pdf. CRS Report R41134, The Impact of Major Legislation on Budget Deficits: 2001 to 2010, by Marc Labonte and Margot L. Crandall-Hollick also examines the reasons why the budget balance changed over time between FY2001, when surpluses were projected by CBO throughout the decade, and FY2010, when the budget deficit was large.

[31] Cutting spending or raising taxes causes the government to borrow less, which results in lower interest payments on the debt. Table 5 includes the effects of lower debt service on the deficit for each policy change; for the discretionary caps, $778 billion of deficit reduction comes from lower discretionary spending and $140 billion comes from lower debt service over 10 years.

[32] Congressional Budget Office, Estimated Impact of Automatic Budget Enforcement Procedures Specified in the Budget Control Act, September 12, 2011.

[33] Mandatory programs enacted on or before the date of enactment of the Balanced Budget Act of 1997 and with estimated outlays of greater than $50 million are assumed to continue in the current year and the outyears for purposes of the baseline.

[34] For more information on the "doc fix" and the cost of extending it, see CRS Report R40907, Medicare Physician Payment Updates and the Sustainable Growth Rate (SGR) System, by Jim Hahn and Janemarie Mulvey.

[35] U.S. Congressional Budget Office, The Budget and Economic Outlook: An Update, August 2011, Table 1-8. Besides these changes, other modifications to the baseline to account for current policy are possible. Besides the AMT and tax cuts, extending other expiring tax provisions would add an additional $920 billion to the budget deficit over 10 years. The baseline could also have included disaster spending at current levels, adjusted for inflation.

[36] For more information, see CRS Report R40770, The Sustainability of the Federal Budget Deficit: Market Confidence and Economic Effects, by Marc Labonte.

[37] Congressional Budget Office, Budget and Economic Outlook: Update, August 2011, p. xv.

[38] For more information, see CRS Report RL32747, The Economic Implications of the Long-Term Federal Budget Outlook, by Marc Labonte.

[39] Economists refer to these policy changes as reducing the structural budget deficit, as opposed to cyclical reductions in the deficit caused by more rapid economic growth.

[40] Reducing the deficit through higher taxes would be expected to have a similar effect on the overall economy.

[41] Theory predicts that the increase in spending from the change in the deficit would be offset by a change in the balance of trade caused by capital flows. By accounting identity, capital flowing into (out of) a country must enter (exit) in the form of a trade deficit (surplus).

[42] For more information, see CRS Report R41849, Can Contractionary Fiscal Policy Be Expansionary?, by Jane G. Gravelle and Thomas L. Hungerford.

[43] These issues are discussed in more detail in CRS Report R40770, The Sustainability of the Federal Budget Deficit: Market Confidence and Economic Effects, by Marc Labonte.

[44] The trade deficit increases because one country can only borrow from another by buying more of the creditor country's goods and services than the creditor buys from the debtor country.

[45] These issues are discussed in more detail in CRS Report R40770, The Sustainability of the Federal Budget Deficit: Market Confidence and Economic Effects, by Marc Labonte.

[46] Reducing the deficit could have positive effects on household and business confidence about the sustainability of fiscal policy that helped the economy. It is not clear that households and businesses currently lack confidence because of future deficits, however, since interest rates on federal debt are unusually low.

[47] JPMorgan, "Let the Pea-Eating Begin," North America Economic Research, newsletter, August 2011. JPMorgan assumes a multiplier of 1 in this calculation, meaning GDP would increase by the same amount as the change in the deficit.

[48] For more information, see CRS Report R41444, Double-Dip Recession: Previous Experience and Current Prospect, by Craig K. Elwell.

[49] Congressional Budget Office, The Budget and Economic Outlook: An Update, August 2011, p. 38.

[50] J.P. Morgan, "Let the Pea-Eating Begin," North America Economic Research, newsletter, August 2011. J.P. Morgan assumes a multiplier of 1 in this calculation, meaning GDP would increase by the same amount as the change in the deficit.

[51] Goldman Sachs, "Some Early Thoughts on Upcoming Fiscal Proposals," U.S. Daily Newsletter, August 19, 2011.

In: The Federal Budget: 2013 and Beyond ISBN: 978-1-62081-920-3
Editors: J. Lambert and I. Johnson

Chapter 4

UPDATED BUDGET PROJECTIONS: FISCAL YEARS 2012 TO 2022*

Congressional Budget Office

INTRODUCTION

In conjunction with its analysis of the President's budget, which will be issued in a few days, the Congressional Budget Office (CBO) has updated the baseline budget projections that it released in January.[1] CBO has not revised its assessment of the economic outlook since January; however, the new baseline projections incorporate the budgetary effects of recently enacted legislation and updated technical assumptions based on new information (such as data about spending and revenues so far this year and program details released in conjunction with the President's budget).

This report summarizes CBO's updated baseline budget projections and describes how they differ from the projections that the agency published two months earlier.[2]

CBO's current estimate of the budget deficit for fiscal year 2012—$1.2 trillion—is $93 billion larger than the deficit projected in January. Conversely, CBO's baseline projection of the cumulative deficit for the 10-year period from 2013 to 2022 is $186 billion smaller than the amount projected in January—a decrease equal to about 0.1 percent of gross domestic product

---

* This is an edited, reformatted and augmented version of Congressional Budget Office publication, dated March 2012.

(GDP) over that period. The fundamental story about the federal budget has not changed: Although the deficit is starting to shrink, it remains very large by historical standards.

How much and how quickly it declines will depend in part on how well the economy performs over the next few years. Probably more critical, though, will be the fiscal policy choices made by lawmakers as they face the substantial changes to tax and spending policies that are slated to take effect within the next year under current law.

CBO's Baseline Budget Projections

As specified in law, and to provide a benchmark against which potential legislation can be measured, CBO constructs its baseline estimates of federal revenues and spending under the assumption that current laws generally remain unchanged.

On that basis, the federal budget is projected to show a deficit of nearly \$1.2 trillion in 2012 (see Table 1). Relative to the nation's gross domestic product, that shortfall will equal 7.6 percent—about 1 percentage point less than the deficit recorded last year but still higher than any deficit between 1946 and 2008. In CBO's baseline, deficits are projected to drop markedly in the next few years and to average 1.4 percent of GDP over the 2013–2022 period.

With deficits small relative to the size of the economy, the amount of federal debt held by the public is projected to drop from nearly 76 percent of GDP in 2013 to 61 percent in 2022—still higher than in any year between 1953 and 2009.

Much of that projected decline occurs because, under current law, revenues will rise considerably as a share of GDP—from 15.8 percent in 2012 to 19.8 percent in 2014 and 21.2 percent in 2022.

In particular, in CBO's baseline, revenues shoot up by more than 30 percent over the next two years, mostly because of the recent or scheduled expirations of tax provisions—such as those that reduce income and payroll tax rates and limit the reach of the alternative minimum tax (AMT)—and the imposition of new taxes, fees, and penalties that are scheduled to go into effect. Revenues are projected to keep rising relative to GDP after 2014 under current law, largely because increases in taxpayers' real (inflation-adjusted) income will push more income into higher tax brackets and because more taxpayers will become subject to the AMT.

(An alternative fiscal scenario, which incorporates the assumptions that almost all expiring tax provisions are extended, that the AMT continues to be indexed for inflation, and that certain other changes are made to current law, is discussed below.)

Federal spending is projected to decline modestly as a percentage of GDP in the next several years under the assumptions of CBO's baseline, as the economy expands and statutory caps constrain discretionary appropriations.

Spending turns upward relative to GDP in later years because of increasing expenses generated by the aging of the population and rising costs for health care.

Outlays are projected to average 22.0 percent of GDP over the 2013–2022 period—lower than the 23.4 percent that CBO estimates for 2012 but still elevated by historical standards. Spending resulting from the American Recovery and Reinvestment Act of 2009 (Public Law 111-5) will continue to ebb over the next few years, as will outlays for unemployment compensation and other benefits that tend to increase during economic downturns. In addition, caps on discretionary spending and other procedures established in the Budget Control Act of 2011 (P.L. 112-25) will hold down the growth of federal outlays.

In the baseline, discretionary spending is projected to decline to 5.6 percent of GDP by 2022—the lowest level in the past 50 years.

The factors constraining outlays will be partially offset by increases in spending for mandatory programs, particularly Social Security, Medicare, Medicaid, and other federal health care programs. In all, mandatory spending is projected to climb from 13.4 percent of GDP in 2013 to 14.3 percent in 2022.[3]

Although the deficits projected under current law are much smaller than the shortfalls seen in the past few years, the federal budget remains out of balance throughout the next decade in CBO's baseline. The resulting accumulation of federal debt, combined with rising interest rates, drives up the projected cost of financing that debt; in CBO's baseline, net interest costs jump from 1.4 percent of GDP this year to 2.5 percent in 2022.

Table 1. CBO's Baseline Budget Projections

	Actual, 2011	2012	2013	2014	2015	2016	2017	2018	2019	2020	2021	2022	Total 2013-2017	Total 2013-2022
						In Billions of Dollars								
Revenues														
Individual income taxes	1,091	1,159	1,465	1,604	1,777	1,927	2,082	2,219	2,364	2,520	2,681	2,849	8,854	21,486
Social insurance taxes	819	825	953	1,020	1,080	1,145	1,213	1,277	1,336	1,397	1,459	1,525	5,410	12,405
Corporate income taxes	181	251	321	386	448	473	467	461	450	449	452	459	2,095	4,365
Other	212	221	230	273	285	293	305	315	333	353	370	385	1,385	3,142
Total	2,303	2,456	2,968	3,283	3,589	3,838	4,066	4,272	4,484	4,719	4,962	5,218	17,744	41,398
On-budget	1,738	1,899	2,293	2,551	2,816	3,016	3,194	3,352	3,519	3,708	3,907	4,115	13,871	32,473
Off-budget[a]	566	556	675	731	773	822	872	919	965	1,011	1,056	1,102	3,873	8,925
Outlays														
Mandatory	2,026	2,101	2,129	2,225	2,361	2,534	2,633	2,742	2,923	3,096	3,283	3,535	11,882	27,462
Discretionary	1,347	1,303	1,219	1,195	1,198	1,220	1,233	1,250	1,283	1,312	1,343	1,381	6,065	12,634
Net interest	230	224	233	248	286	343	401	454	503	544	573	604	1,511	4,189
Total	3,603	3,627	3,580	3,668	3,846	4,097	4,267	4,447	4,708	4,953	5,200	5,520	19,457	44,285
On-budget	3,104	3,124	2,941	2,959	3,091	3,296	3,417	3,547	3,754	3,939	4,123	4,377	15,704	35,443
Off-budget[a]	499	503	639	709	755	801	850	900	954	1,014	1,077	1,143	3,754	8,841
Deficit (-) or Surplus	-1,300	-1,171	-612	-385	-257	-259	-201	-175	-224	-234	-237	-303	-1,713	-2,887
On-budget	-1,367	-1,224	-647	-408	-275	-279	-223	-194	-235	-231	-216	-262	-1,833	-2,971
Off-budget[a]	67	53	36	23	18	21	22	19	11	-3	-21	-41	119	84
Debt Held by the Public	10,128	11,347	12,068	12,556	12,909	13,263	13,560	13,820	14,123	14,432	14,741	15,115	n.a.	n.a.
Memorandum:														
Gross Domestic Product	14,954	15,508	15,914	16,575	17,618	18,704	19,708	20,661	21,616	22,603	23,614	24,655	88,519	201,666
					As a Percentage of Gross Domestic Product									
Revenues														
Individual income taxes	7.3	7.5	9.2	9.7	10.1	10.3	10.6	10.7	10.9	11.1	11.4	11.6	10.0	10.7
Social insurance taxes	5.5	5.3	6.0	6.2	6.1	6.1	6.2	6.2	6.2	6.2	6.2	6.2	6.1	6.2
Corporate income taxes	1.2	1.6	2.0	2.3	2.5	2.5	2.4	2.2	2.1	2.0	1.9	1.9	2.4	2.2
Other	1.4	1.4	1.4	1.6	1.6	1.6	1.5	1.5	1.5	1.6	1.6	1.6	1.6	1.6
Total	15.4	15.8	18.7	19.8	20.4	20.5	20.6	20.7	20.7	20.9	21.0	21.2	20.0	20.5

												Total	
	Actual,											2013-	2013-
	2011	2012	2013	2014	2015	2016	2017	2018	2019	2020	2021	2022	2017	2022
						In Billions of Dollars							
On-budget	11.6	12.2	14.4	15.4	16.0	16.1	16.2	16.2	16.3	16.4	16.5	16.7	15.7	16.1
Off-budget[a]	3.8	3.6	4.2	4.4	4.4	4.4	4.4	4.4	4.5	4.5	4.5	4.5	4.4	4.4
Outlays														
Mandatory	13.6	13.5	13.4	13.4	13.4	13.5	13.4	13.3	13.5	13.7	13.9	14.3	13.4	13.6
Discretionary	9.0	8.4	7.7	7.2	6.8	6.5	6.3	6.1	5.9	5.8	5.7	5.6	6.9	6.3
Net interest	1.5	1.4	1.5	1.5	1.6	1.8	2.0	2.2	2.3	2.4	2.4	2.5	1.7	2.1
Total	24.1	23.4	22.5	22.1	21.8	21.9	21.7	21.5	21.8	21.9	22.0	22.4	22.0	22.0
On-budget	20.8	20.1	18.5	17.9	17.5	17.6	17.3	17.2	17.4	17.4	17.5	17.8	17.7	17.6
Off-budget[a]	3.3	3.2	4.0	4.3	4.3	4.3	4.3	4.4	4.4	4.5	4.6	4.6	4.2	4.4
Deficit (-) or Surplus	-8.7	-7.6	-3.8	-2.3	-1.5	-1.4	-1.0	-0.8	-1.0	-1.0	-1.0	-1.2	-1.9	-1.4
On-budget	-9.1	-7.9	-4.1	-2.5	-1.6	-1.5	-1.1	-0.9	-1.1	-1.0	-0.9	-1.1	-2.1	-1.5
Off-budget[a]	0.4	0.3	0.2	0.1	0.1	0.1	0.1	0.1	*	*	-0.1	-0.2	0.1	*
Debt Held by the Public	67.7	73.2	75.8	75.8	73.3	70.9	68.8	66.9	65.3	63.9	62.4	61.3	n.a.	n.a.

Source: Congressional Budget Office.

Note: n.a. = not applicable; * = between -0.05 percent and 0.05 percent.

[a]. Off-budget surpluses or deficits comprise surpluses or deficits in the Social Security trust funds and the net cash flow of the Postal Service.

Table 2. Deficits Projected in CBO's Baseline and Under an Alternative Fiscal Scenario

											Total	
	2012	2013	2014	2015	2016	2017	2018	2019	2020	2021	2022	2013-2017	2013-2022
						In Billions of Dollars							
						CBO's March 2012 Baseline							
Revenues	2,456	2,968	3,283	3,589	3,838	4,066	4,272	4,484	4,719	4,962	5,218	17,744	41,398
Outlays	3,627	3,580	3,668	3,846	4,097	4,267	4,447	4,708	4,953	5,200	5,520	19,457	44,285

Table 2. (Continued)

												Total	
	2012	2013	2014	2015	2016	2017	2018	2019	2020	2021	2022	2013-2017	2013-2022
						In Billions of Dollars							
						CBO's March 2012 Baseline							
Deficit	-1,171	-612	-385	-257	-259	-201	-175	-224	-234	-237	-303	-1,713	-2,887
Debt Held by the Public at the End of the Year	11,347	12,068	12,556	12,909	13,263	13,560	13,820	14,123	14,432	14,741	15,115	n.a.	n.a.
						Alternative Fiscal Scenario							
Revenues	2,432	2,660	2,873	3,147	3,378	3,583	3,760	3,943	4,139	4,341	4,550	15,641	36,374
Outlays	3,627	3,660	3,826	4,030	4,312	4,520	4,739	5,046	5,338	5,635	5,999	20,348	47,105
Deficit	-1,195	-1,000	-953	-883	-934	-936	-979	-1,104	-1,199	-1,294	-1,449	-4,707	-10,731
Debt Held by the Public at the End of the Year	11,370	12,479	13,536	14,515	15,545	16,577	17,641	18,823	20,098	21,462	22,983	n.a.	n.a.
						As a Percentage of Gross Domestic Product CBO's March 2012 Baseline							
Revenues	15.8	18.7	19.8	20.4	20.5	20.6	20.7	20.7	20.9	21.0	21.2	20.0	20.5
Outlays	23.4	22.5	22.1	21.8	21.9	21.7	21.5	21.8	21.9	22.0	22.4	22.0	22.0
Deficit	-7.6	-3.8	-2.3	-1.5	-1.4	-1.0	-0.8	-1.0	-1.0	-1.0	-1.2	-1.9	-1.4
Debt Held by the Public at the End of the Year	73.2	75.8	75.8	73.3	70.9	68.8	66.9	65.3	63.9	62.4	61.3	n.a.	n.a.
						Alternative Fiscal Scenario							
Revenues	15.7	16.7	17.3	17.9	18.1	18.2	18.2	18.2	18.3	18.4	18.5	17.7	18.0
Outlays	23.4	23.0	23.1	22.9	23.1	22.9	22.9	23.3	23.6	23.9	24.3	23.0	23.4
Deficit	-7.7	-6.3	-5.8	-5.0	-5.0	-4.8	-4.7	-5.1	-5.3	-5.5	-5.9	-5.3	-5.3
Debt Held by the Public at the End of the Year	73.3	78.4	81.7	82.4	83.1	84.1	85.4	87.1	88.9	90.9	93.2	n.a.	n.a.

												Total	
	2012	2013	2014	2015	2016	2017	2018	2019	2020	2021	2022	2013-2017	2013-2022
						In Billions of Dollars							
Memorandum: Deficit: Alternative Fiscal Scenario Minus CBO's March 2012 Baseline In billions of dollars	-23	-388	-568	-627	-676	-736	-804	-879	-965	-1,056	-1,147	-2,994	-7,845
As a percentage of GDP	-0.2	-2.4	-3.4	-3.6	-3.6	-3.7	-3.9	-4.1	-4.3	-4.5	-4.7	-3.4	-3.9
Policy Alternatives That Affect the Tax Code (Billions of dollars)													
Effect on revenues	-23	-309	-410	-442	-460	-483	-511	-541	-579	-621	-668	-2,104	-5,024
Effect on outlays	0	1	39	41	42	43	43	43	42	42	42	166	378
Effect on the deficita	-23	-309	-449	-483	-502	-526	-554	-584	-622	-663	-710	-2,270	-5,403

Source: Congressional Budget Office.

Notes: The alternative fiscal scenario incorporates the assumptions that all expiring tax provisions (other than the payroll tax reduction), including those that expired at the end of December 2011, are instead extended; that the alternative minimum tax is indexed for inflation after 2011 (starting at the 2011 exemption amount); that Medicare's payment rates for physicians' services are held constant at their current level; and that the automatic enforcement procedures specified by the Budget Control Act of 2011 do not take effect. Outlays under the alternative fiscal scenario also include the incremental interest costs associated with projected additional borrowing.

n.a. = not applicable; GDP = gross domestic product. a. Negative numbers indicate an increase in the deficit.

Budget Projections Under an Alternative Fiscal Scenario

CBO's baseline projections are heavily influenced by changes in tax and spending policies that are embodied in current law—changes that in some cases represent a significant departure from recent policies. As a result, thoseprojections show much higher revenues and lower outlays than would occur if the lower tax rates that are now in effect were extended and if provisions that limit future spending were eased. To illustrate the budgetary consequences of maintaining the tax and spending policies that have recently been in effect, CBO has also produced projections under an "alternative fiscal scenario." That scenario incorporates the following assumptions:

- Expiring tax provisions (other than the current reduction in the payroll tax rate for Social Security) are extended;
- The AMT is indexed for inflation after 2011;
- Medicare's payment rates for physicians' services are held constant at their current level (rather than dropping by an estimated 27 percent in January 2013 and more thereafter, as scheduled under current law); and
- The automatic spending reductions required by the Budget Control Act, which are set to take effect in January 2013, do not occur (although the original caps on discretionary appropriations in that law are assumed to remain in place).

Under that alternative fiscal scenario, deficits over the 2013–2022 period would be much higher, averaging 5.3 percent of GDP rather than the 1.4 percent reflected in CBO's baseline projections (see Table 2 and Figure 1). Instead of declining to 61 percent of GDP, debt held by the public would climb to 93 percent in 2022, the highest percentage since just after World War II (see Figure 2).

Over the longer term, budgetary challenges will remain even if the fiscal policies specified by current law come to pass—and the challenges will be much more acute if those policies do not remain in place. Under both CBO's baseline and its alternative fiscal scenario, the aging of the population and rising costs for health care will push spending for Social Security, Medicare, Medicaid, and other federal health care programs considerably higher as a percentage of GDP. If that rising level of spending is coupled with revenues that are held close to their average percentage of GDP for the past 40 years (rather than being allowed to increase, as under current law), the resulting deficits will push federal debt to unsupportable levels. To prevent that outcome, policymakers will have to substantially restrain the growth of spending for those programs, raise revenues above their historical share of GDP, or pursue some combination of those two approaches.

CHANGES IN CBO'S BASELINE PROJECTIONS SINCE JANUARY 2012

The recent revisions to CBO's baseline projections include estimates of the effects of legislation enacted in the past two months as well as so-called technical changes—revisions that occur for reasons other than new laws or updated economic information. (As it typically does for its March baseline projections, CBO has used the same set of economic assumptions developed for the January baseline.) CBO now estimates that, without further changes to tax and spending laws, the deficit for 2012 will be $93 billion larger than the $1.1 trillion figure projected in January; however, CBO's new baseline projections show a cumulative deficit for the following 10 years that is $186 billion smaller than the $3.1 trillion total projected in January. As a result, CBO now projects deficits totaling about $2.9 trillion over the 2013–2022 period under the assumptions of the baseline. In contrast, under the alternative fiscal scenario described above, deficits would total $10.7 trillion over that period (about $250 billion less than CBO projected in January for that scenario).

The changes in the outlook for 2012 since January stem almost entirely from the enactment of legislation, which added $100 billion to the estimated deficit for this year. In contrast, the changes in the projections for the 2013– 2022 period result mainly from technical estimating revisions, which have reduced projected deficits over those years by a total of $208 billion (see Table 3).

Legislative Changes

CBO and the staff of the Joint Committee on Taxation (JCT) estimate that recent legislative actions will increase deficits by $100 billion in 2012 and by $22 billion over the 2013–2022 period. Nearly all of that effect comes from enactment of the Middle Class Tax Relief and Job Creation Act of 2012 (P.L. 112-96).

Among its revenue provisions, P.L. 112-96 extended for 10 months (through December 2012) the 2 percentage-point cut in the payroll tax rate for Social Security that first went into effect in January 2011; that extension reduces projected revenues by an estimated $70 billion in 2012 and $23 billion in 2013. Starting in January 2013, P.L. 112-96 will require future federal employees to make larger contributions to their retirement plan, adding $15 billion to projected revenues over the 2013–2022 period. In addition, the law repealed a number of scheduled changes to rules governing the timing of estimated tax payments by corporations; the most significant of those repeals is projected to reduce revenues by $42 billion in 2014 and increase them by the same amount during the 2015–2017 period.

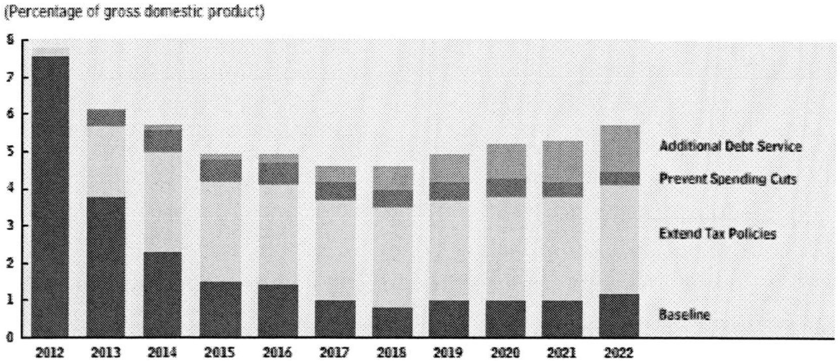

Source: Congressional Budget Office.

Note: "Extend Tax Policies" reflects the assumptions in the alternative fiscal scenario that expiring tax provisions (other than the payroll tax reduction) are instead extended and that the alternative minimum tax is indexed for inflation. "Prevent Spending Cuts" involves holding Medicare's payment rates for physicians' services at their current level (rather than permitting them to drop, as scheduled under current law) and preventing the cuts to federal spending that will occur under the automatic enforcement procedures of the Budget Control Act of 2011 from taking effect (but leaving in place the original caps on discretionary appropriations in that law).

"Additional Debt Service" is the amount of interest payments on the additional debt issued to the public that would result from those policies in the alternative fiscal scenario.

Figure 1. Deficits Projected in CBO's Baseline and Under an Alternative Fiscal Scenario.

Enactment of P.L. 112-96 also affects outlays. The law extended emergency unemployment benefits through December 2012, at an estimated total cost of $30 billion in 2012 and 2013. It also temporarily delayed a scheduled reduction in Medicare's payment rates for physicians and made other changes to the Medicare program, at a net cost of $10 billion over the 2012–2022 period. In the other direction, P.L. 112-96 authorized new auctions of licenses to use the electromagnetic spectrum, which (after accounting for the spending of some of the auction receipts) will lower net outlays by $15 billion over the next 10 years. Other, smaller effects of the new law include certain cuts in federal spending for health care (such as a $5 billion reduction in spending by the Prevention and Public Health Fund over the 2013–2022 period) and a decrease of $3 billion over 10 years in the Postal Service's contributions for its employees' retirement (for employees who start in 2013 or later).

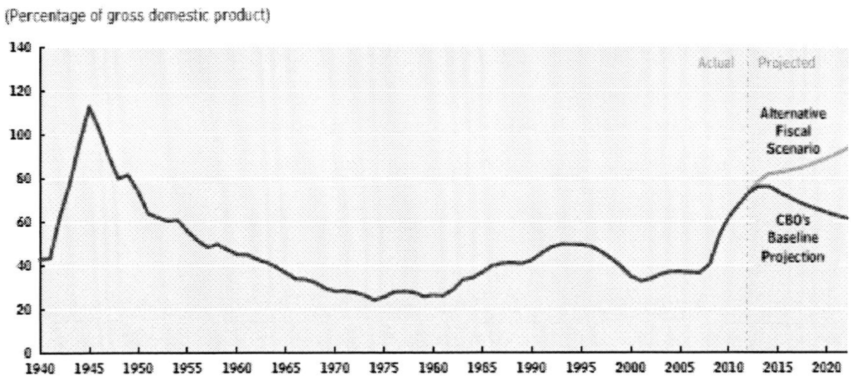

Source: Congressional Budget Office.

Note: The alternative fiscal scenario incorporates the assumptions that all expiring tax provisions (other than the payroll tax reduction), including those that expired at the end of December 2011, are instead extended; that the alternative minimum tax is indexed for inflation after 2011 (starting at the 2011 exemption amount); that Medicare's payment rates for physicians' services are held constant at their current level; and that the automatic enforcement procedures specified by the Budget Control Act of 2011 do not take effect. The budgetary effects under the alternative fiscal scenario also include the incremental interest costs associated with projected additional borrowing.

Figure 2. Federal Debt Held by the Public Projected in CBO's Baseline and Under an Alternative Fiscal Scenario.

All told, the effects of P.L. 112-96—combined with minor budgetary effects of other legislation—add $100 billion to the estimated deficit for 2012 and decrease projected deficits by $10 billion over the 2013– 2022 period (the net result of a $17 billion reduction in mandatory spending and a $7 billion reduction in revenues).

As a result, federal borrowing and interest payments on federal debt will be greater than they would be without the new legislation. CBO estimates that interest payments on that additional borrowing will boost deficits by another $32 billion between 2013 and 2022.

Technical Changes

Overall, technical updates have lowered CBO's estimate of the deficit in 2012 by $7 billion and its baseline projections of deficits for the following 10 years by a total of $208 billion. Increases in projected revenues—totaling $3 billion in 2012 and $226 billion over the 2013–2022 period—represent the largest changes. For both revenues and outlays, the most significant technical revisions stem from updated estimates for the insurance coverage provisions of the Affordable Care Act (ACA).[4] (For more details about those revisions, see Congressional Budget Office, *Updated Estimates for the Insurance Coverage Provisions of the Affordable Care Act*, issued on March 13, 2012.)

Revenues. Updates to estimates for the ACA's health care provisions account for most of the $229 billion increase in projected revenues between 2012 and 2022 attributable to technical factors. CBO and JCT have lowered their estimates of the number of people who will receive health insurance coverage through an employer and the number of people who will receive such coverage through newly established insurance exchanges. As a result of those and other changes, CBO's current baseline incorporates lower projections of tax credits for individuals who purchase health insurance through the exchanges and for small businesses that provide health insurance to their employees, as well as higher projections of penalty payments by people who do not obtain health insurance and businesses that do not provide it. Moreover, because fewer employers are expected to contribute to premium payments for their employees' health insurance (such payments are not subject to individual income or payroll taxes), a larger share of total compensation is now expected to be in the form of wages and salaries (which are subject to taxation). CBO's baseline projections include additional revenues from that shift in the composition of taxable compensation.

Outlays. Technical updates since January have had only small net effects on CBO's spending projections, reducing estimated outlays in 2012 by $4 billion and increasing projected outlays over the 2013–2022 period by a total of $19 billion. Over that 10-year period, higher projected spending for Medicaid is mostly offset by lower projected spending for Social Security and net interest.

CBO has boosted its projection of Medicaid outlays over the 2013–2022 period by a total of $143 billion (or 3 percent). That change stems in part from an increase in CBO and JCT's estimate of the number of low-income people who will qualify for Medicaid under the ACA and from an increase in the projected federal share of costs for those who enroll.[5] Other, smaller effects result from incorporating updated information about enrollment and spending for components of Medicaid.

CBO has reduced its projection of outlays for Social Security over the 2013–2022 period by $26 billion (or 0.2 percent) for technical reasons. CBO now estimates that the number of people receiving benefits under Social Security's Old-Age and Survivors Insurance program will be slightly smaller than previously projected, whereas the average benefit will be slightly larger.

In addition, CBO now expects average award amounts for new beneficiaries in Social Security's Disability Insurance program to grow more slowly than previously projected.

Other changes include a $7 billion reduction in projected spending for Medicare over the 2013–2022 period. That decrease results from a $107 billion reduction in projected spending for prescription drug benefits under Part D of Medicare—primarily reflecting an increase in the number of high-volume drugs with generic substitutes available and changes in drug utilization—largely offset by increases in projected spending for benefits covered under Parts A (hospital insurance) and B (medical insurance) of Medicare. In its projections for Parts A and B, CBO has increased the Medicare Advantage program's share of both enrollment and spending. In its previous baseline, CBO anticipated that enrollment in Medicare Advantage plans would decline from 11.2 million people in 2013 to 8.7 million in 2021. Because of unanticipated increases in enrollment for 2012 (and an expectation that enrollment will remain higher than previously estimated), CBO now projects that enrollment in those plans will total 13.3 million in 2013 and about 11 million in both 2021 and 2022.

Technical changes have directly lowered CBO's estimate of net interest costs over the 2013–2022 period by $49 billion. Most of that decrease is attributable to a shift in the mix of securities that the Treasury is expected to issue (from longer-term securities and inflation-protected securities to short-term securities), partly offset by lower projections of interest receipts unrelated to Treasury borrowing.

Table 3. Changes in CBO's Baseline Projections of the Deficit Since January 2012

(Billions of dollars)													
												Total	
												2013-2017	2013-2022
	2012	2013	2014	2015	2016	2017	2018	2019	2020	2021	2022		
Deficit in CBO's January 2012 Baseline	-1,079	-585	-345	-269	-302	-220	-196	-258	-280	-279	-339	-1,721	-3,072
						Legislative Changes							
Changes in Revenues	-70	-23	-42	5	37	4	2	-2	7	3	3	-19	-7
Changes in Outlays													
Mandatory outlays													
Unemployment compensation	20	10	*	*	*	*	*	*	*	*	*	10	10
Medicare	9	5	-1	-1	*	*	*	*	*	-1	-1	3	1
Spectrum auctions	0	3	*	-3	-4	-4	-3	-2	-1	-1	*	-8	-15
Other	*	1	-1	-2	-1	-1	-1	-1	-1	-5	-1	-5	-14
Subtotal	29	19	-2	-6	-5	-5	-4	-4	-2	-7	-1	1	-17
Debt service	*	1	2	3	3	3	4	4	4	4	5	11	32
All Changes in Outlays	30	20	-1	-3	-2	-2	-1	*	2	-2	3	12	15
Total Legislative Changes[a]	-100	-43	-41	8	38	6	2	-3	5	5	*	-31	-22
						Technical Changes							
Changes in Revenues	3	3	11	17	17	23	26	30	32	33	33	71	226
Changes in Outlays													
Mandatory outlays													
Medicaid	-4	-5	8	15	18	19	18	19	18	17	17	54	143
Social Security	-1	-1	-1	-1	-2	-2	-3	-3	-4	-4	-6	-7	-26
Other	6	-6	5	-1	-3	-2	2	-7	-5	5	11	-7	-1
Subtotal	2	-13	12	12	14	15	18	8	9	18	23	40	116

(Billions of dollars)													
												Total	
												2013-2017	2013-2022
	2012	2013	2014	2015	2016	2017	2018	2019	2020	2021	2022		
Discretionary outlays	-5	-1	-1	-1	*	*	-1	-1	-1	-1	*	-3	-7
Net interest													
Debt service	*	*	*	-1	-2	-2	-3	-5	-7	-9	-11	-5	-41
Other	-1	1	*	2	*	-2	-5	-9	-11	-12	-13	1	-49
Subtotal	-1	1	*	1	-1	-4	-9	-14	-18	-21	-25	-4	-90
All Changes in Outlays	-4	-13	10	12	12	10	8	-6	-10	-3	-3	32	19
Total Technical Changes[a]	7	16	1	4	5	13	18	36	42	37	36	39	208
						All Changes							
Total Impact on the Deficit[a]	-93	-27	-40	12	43	19	21	34	46	42	36	8	186
Revenues	-67	-20	-31	21	54	27	28	28	39	36	37	52	219
Outlays	-26	-7	-10	-9	-10	-8	-8	6	7	6	-1	-44	-33
Deficit in CBO's March 2012 Baseline	-1,171	-612	-385	-257	-259	-201	-175	-224	-234	-237	-303	-1,713	-2,887

Source: Congressional Budget Office.

Note: * = between -$500 million and $500 million.

[a]. Negative numbers indicate an increase in the deficit, and positive numbers indicate a decrease.

In addition, because the various technical changes described above have reduced CBO's estimate of the deficit in 2012 by $7 billion and its baseline deficit projections for the 2013–2022 period by $167 billion, the amount of debt held by the public is now projected to be smaller than it would be otherwise. That change in debt reduces projected debt-service costs by a total of $41 billion between 2013 and 2020, bringing the total decrease in baseline deficits over that period because of technical changes to $208 billion.

End Notes

[1]. Those projections were published in Congressional Budget Office, The Budget and Economic Outlook: Fiscal Years 2012 to 2022 (January 2012).

[2]. Supplemental information about CBO's new baseline is available on the agency's Web site (www.cbo.gov).

[3]. Because of a shift in the timing of certain payments, projected mandatory spending in 2022 is about $42 billion (or 0.2 percent of GDP) higher than it would be otherwise.

[4]. As used in this report, ACA refers to the Patient Protection and Affordable Care Act (P.L. 111-148) and the amendments made to that law by the health care provisions of the Health Care and Education Reconciliation Act of 2010 (P.L. 111-152). CBO and JCT did not complete the process of updating their 2011 estimates of the budgetary effects of the ACA's provisions related to health insurance coverage in time for the January 2012 Budget and Economic Outlook. Thus, the updated estimates for the ACA described here reflect changes in CBO's economic forecast since January 2011 as well as technical changes made since early 2011.

[5]. The change in projected spending for Medicaid reported here differs from the change shown in CBO's report Updated Estimates for the Insurance Coverage Provisions of the Affordable Care Act. The change discussed here applies to projected outlays for the entire Medicaid program—not just the outlays related to the ACA—and it encompasses revisions made to the projections between January and March 2012. CBO's report on estimates of the insurance coverage provisions of the ACA deals only with that legislation and compares the estimates in the March 2012 baseline with estimates from the March 2011 baseline—the last time that detailed information about CBO and JCT's estimates of the coverage provisions of the ACA was published.

In: The Federal Budget: 2013 and Beyond ISBN: 978-1-62081-920-3
Editors: J. Lambert and I. Johnson

Chapter 5

AN ANALYSIS OF THE PRESIDENT'S 2013 BUDGET*

Congressional Budget Office

NOTES

Unless otherwise indicated, the years referred to in this report are federal fiscal years (which run from October 1 to September 30).

Numbers in the text and tables may not add up to totals because of rounding.

Supplemental information about this analysis is available on CBO's Web site (www.cbo.gov).

OVERVIEW

This report by the Congressional Budget Office (CBO) presents an analysis of the proposals contained in the President's budget request for fiscal year 2013.

---

* This is an edited, reformatted and augmented version of a Congressional Budget Office publication, dated March 2012.

The analysis is based on CBO's economic projections and estimating techniques (rather than the Administration's) and incorporates estimates by the staff of the Joint Committee on Taxation for the President's tax proposals.[1]

In conjunction with analyzing the President's budget, CBO has updated its baseline budget projections, which were previously issued in January 2012. Unlike its estimates of the President's budget, CBO's baseline projections largely reflect the assumption that current tax and spending laws will remain unchanged, so as to provide a benchmark against which potential legislation can be measured. Under that assumption, CBO estimates that the deficit would total $1.2 trillion in 2012 and that cumulative deficits over the 2013–2022 period would amount to $2.9 trillion.[2]

The President's budget request specifies spending and revenue policies for the 2013–2022 period and also includes initiatives that would have budgetary effects in fiscal year 2012.[3]

CBO estimates that enactment of the President's proposals would have the following consequences for the budget:

- The deficit in 2012 would equal $1.3 trillion (or 8.1 percent of gross domestic product), $82 billion more than the 2012 deficit projected in CBO's baseline.
- In 2013, the deficit would decline to $977 billion (or 6.1 percent of GDP), $365 billion more than the shortfall projected for 2013 in CBO's baseline.
- The deficit would decline further relative to GDP in subsequent years, reaching 2.5 percent by 2017, but then would increase again, reaching 3.0 percent of GDP in 2022. The deficits after 2013 would exceed those in CBO's baseline by between 1.4 percent and 1.9 percent of GDP each year (see Table 1).
- In all, between 2013 and 2022, deficits would total $6.4 trillion (or 3.2 percent of total GDP projected for that period), $3.5 trillion more than the cumulative deficit in CBO's baseline.
- Federal debt held by the public would increase from $10.1 trillion (68 percent of GDP) at the end of 2011 to $15.2 trillion (77 percent of GDP) at the end of 2017 and then to $18.8 trillion (76 percent of GDP) at the end of 2022 (see Table 2). Under the assumptions of CBO's current-law baseline, debt held by the public would increase more slowly, ending 2022 at $15.1 trillion; as a percentage of GDP, however, such debt would decline to 61 percent by the end of 2022.

Table 1. Comparison of Projected Revenues, Outlays, and Deficits Under CBO's March 2012 Baseline and in CBO's Estimate of the President's Budget (Billions of dollars)

	Actual, 2011	2012	2013	2014	2015	2016	2017	2018	2019	2020	2021	2022	Total 2013-2017	Total 2013-2022
						TotalCBO's March 2012 Baseline								
Revenues	2,303	2,456	2,968	3,283	3,589	3,838	4,066	4,272	4,484	4,719	4,962	5,218	17,44	41,398
Outlays	3,603	3,627	3,580	3,668	3,846	4,097	4,267	4,447	4,708	4,953	5,200	5,520	19,457	44,285
Total Deficit	-1,300	-1,171	-612	-385	-257	-259	-201	-175	-224	-234	-237	-303	-1,713	-2,887
						CBO's Estimate of the President's Budget								
Revenues	2,303	2,394	2,741	3,105	3,413	3,657	3,868	4,043	4,227	4,445	4,661	4,885	16,783	39,044
Outlays	3,603	3,647	3,717	3,807	3,952	4,186	4,356	4,553	4,829	5,083	5,339	5,613	20,018	45,434
Total Deficit	-1,300	-1,253	-977	-702	-539	-529	-488	-510	-602	-638	-678	-728	-3,235	-6,390
			Difference Between CBO's Estimate of the President's Budget and CBO's Baseline											
Revenues	n.a.	61	-228	-178	-176	-181	-198	-229	-256	-274	-301	-333	-961	-2,354
Outlays	n.a.	20	137	139	106	90	89	106	121	131	139	92	561	1,150
Total Deficit	n.a.	-82	-365	-317	-282	-270	-287	-335	-377	-404	-440	-425	-1,522	-3,504
Memorandum:														
Deficit as a Percentage of GDP														
CBO's baseline	-8.7	-7.6	-3.8	-2.3	-1.5	-1.4	-1.0	-0.8	-1.0	-1.0	-1.0	-1.2	-1.9	-1.4
CBO's estimate of the President's budget	-8.7	-8.1	-6.1	-4.2	-3.1	-2.8	-2.5	-2.5	-2.8	-2.8	-2.9	-3.0	-3.7	-3.2
Debt Held by the Public as a Percentage of GDP														

Table 1. (Continued)

	Actual, 2011	2012	2013	2014	2015	2016	2017	2018	2019	2020	2021	2022	Total 2013-2017	Total 2013-2022
CBO's baseline	67.7	73.2	75.8	75.8	73.3	70.9	68.8	66.9	65.3	63.9	62.4	61.3	n.a.	n.a.
CBO's estimate of the President's budget	67.7	73.7	78.7	80.4	79.4	78.2	77.2	76.6	76.4	76.3	76.3	76.3	n.a.	n.a.

Sources: Congressional Budget Office; Staff of the Joint Committee on Taxation.

Note: n.a. = not applicable; GDP = gross domestic product.

[a] Negative numbers indicate an increase in the deficit relative to CBO's baseline.

Table 2. CBO's Estimate of the President's Budget

	Actual, 2011	2012	2013	2014	2015	2016	2017	2018	2019	2020	2021	2022	Total 2013-2017	Total 2013-2022
						In Billions of Dollars								
Revenues														
On-budget	1,738	1,838	2,066	2,374	2,641	2,836	2,996	3,124	3,263	3,435	3,606	3,783	12,912	30,123
Off-budget[a]	566	556	675	731	772	821	872	919	965	1,010	1,055	1,102	3,871	8,921
Total	2,303	2,394	2,741	3,105	3,413	3,657	3,868	4,043	4,227	4,445	4,661	4,885	16,783	39,044
Outlays														
Mandatory	2,026	2,119	2,221	2,368	2,497	2,659	2,756	2,869	3,050	3,217	3,399	3,588	12,501	28,624
Discretionary	1,347	1,303	1,259	1,183	1,155	1,158	1,158	1,170	1,198	1,225	1,248	1,282	5,914	12,035
Net interest	230	225	237	255	300	370	442	513	581	642	692	743	1,604	4,775
Total	3,603	3,647	3,717	3,807	3,952	4,186	4,356	4,553	4,829	5,083	5,339	5,613	20,018	45,434
On-budget	3,104	3,144	3,078	3,098	3,197	3,386	3,507	3,654	3,876	4,071	4,264	4,472	16,266	36,603
Off-budget[a]	499	504	639	708	755	800	849	899	953	1,012	1,075	1,141	3,752	8,832

	Actual, 2011	2012	2013	2014	2015	2016	2017	2018	2019	2020	2021	2022	Total 2013-2017	Total 2013-2022
						In Billions of Dollars								
Deficit (-) or Surplus	-1,300	-1,253	-977	-702	-539	-529	-488	-510	-602	-638	-678	-728	-3,235	-6,390
On-budget	-1,367	-1,306	-1,012	-725	-556	-550	-511	-530	-613	-636	-658	-689	-3,354	-6,480
Off-budget[a]	67	53	36	23	18	21	22	20	12	-2	-20	-39	119	90
Debt Held by the Public	10,128	11,427	12,517	13,331	13,982	14,618	15,215	15,825	16,519	17,246	18,007	18,819	n.a.	n.a.
Memorandum:														
Gross Domestic Product	14,954	15,508	15,914	16,575	17,618	18,704	19,708	20,661	21,616	22,603	23,614	24,655	88,519	201,666
					As a Percentage of Gross Domestic Product									
Revenues														
On-budget	11.6	11.9	13.0	14.3	15.0	15.2	15.2	15.1	15.1	15.2	15.3	15.3	14.6	14.9
Off-budget[a]	3.8	3.6	4.2	4.4	4.4	4.4	4.4	4.4	4.5	4.5	4.5	4.5	4.4	4.4
Total	15.4	15.4	17.2	18.7	19.4	19.6	19.6	19.6	19.6	19.7	19.7	19.8	19.0	19.4
Outlays														
Mandatory spending	13.6	13.7	14.0	14.3	14.2	14.2	14.0	13.9	14.1	14.2	14.4	14.6	14.1	14.2
Discretionary spending	9.0	8.4	7.9	7.1	6.6	6.2	5.9	5.7	5.5	5.4	5.3	5.2	6.7	6.0
Net interest	1.5	1.5	1.5	1.5	1.7	2.0	2.2	2.5	2.7	2.8	2.9	3.0	1.8	2.4
Total	24.1	23.5	23.4	23.0	22.4	22.4	22.1	22.0	22.3	22.5	22.6	22.8	22.6	22.5
On-budget	20.8	20.3	19.3	18.7	18.1	18.1	17.8	17.7	17.9	18.0	18.1	18.1	18.4	18.2
Off-budget[a]	3.3	3.2	4.0	4.3	4.3	4.3	4.3	4.4	4.4	4.5	4.6	4.6	4.2	4.4
Deficit (-) or Surplus	-8.7	-8.1	-6.1	-4.2	-3.1	-2.8	-2.5	-2.5	-2.8	-2.8	-2.9	-3.0	-3.7	-3.2
On-budget	-9.1	-8.4	-6.4	-4.4	-3.2	-2.9	-2.6	-2.6	-2.8	-2.8	-2.8	-2.8	-3.8	-3.2
Off-budget[a]	0.4	0.3	0.2	0.1	0.1	0.1	0.1	0.1	0.1	*	-0.1	-0.2	0.1	*
Debt Held by the Public	67.7	73.7	78.7	80.4	79.4	78.2	77.2	76.6	76.4	76.3	76.3	76.3	n.a.	n.a.

Sources: Congressional Budget Office; Staff of the Joint Committee on Taxation.

Note: n.a. = not applicable; * = between -0.05 percent and 0.05 percent.

[a]. Off-budget surpluses or deficits comprise surpluses or deficits in the Social Security trust funds and the net cash flow of the Postal Service.

The President's budget contains a host of proposed changes to spending and revenue policies. By CBO's estimate, those policy changes would, on net, add about $2.9 trillion to projected deficits over the 2013–2022 period and necessitate $0.6 trillion in additional interest payments (because of increased federal borrowing). Most of the net budgetary impact would come from changes in tax policies, but changes in spending policies would also play a role:

- The President proposes to extend certain tax provisions that are slated to expire or that have already expired. The 2010 tax act (officially the Tax Relief, Unemployment Insurance Reauthorization, and Job Creation Act of 2010, Public Law 111-312) extended through December 2012 many of the income tax reductions originally enacted in the Economic Growth and Tax Relief Reconciliation Act of 2001 (EGTRRA) and the Jobs and Growth Tax Relief Reconciliation Act of 2003 (JGTRRA). The President proposes to make those reductions permanent—except, in some cases, for higher-income taxpayers. In addition, the President seeks to reduce the number of taxpayers who would be subject to the alternative minimum tax (AMT) by permanently setting various parameters of that tax at the amounts that were in effect in calendar year 2011 and indexing those amounts for inflation in later years. The President also proposes, starting in January 2013, to permanently restore the rates and exemption levels for estate and gift taxes that were in effect in calendar year 2009. Together, those policies would reduce tax revenues and boost outlays for refundable tax credits by a total of about $3.5 trillion over the 2013–2022 period relative to the amounts projected in CBO's baseline.[4]
- Automatic procedures specified by last year's Budget Control Act (P.L. 112-25) are set to go into effect in January 2013 and reduce spending in subsequent years.[5] The President's budget does not include those reductions, thereby boosting outlays relative to the current-law baseline by $1.0 trillion over the next 10 years.
- The President is also proposing some policies that would reduce projected deficits relative to CBO's baseline. For example, the President's budget envisions funding for military operations in Afghanistan and for related activities (also known as overseas contingency operations, or OCO) that is less than the amounts in CBO's baseline. As specified in law, the baseline incorporates the

assumption that funding for such activities will total $127 billion (the amount provided in 2012) each year through 2022, with increases to keep pace with inflation; the President's budget, by comparison, includes a request for $97 billion for OCO in 2013 and $44 billion in each year thereafter through 2022. The cumulative difference in outlays between CBO's baseline and the President's proposal is $0.8 trillion over the 2013–2022 period.

- The President would also cap the rate at which certain deductions and exclusions reduce a taxpayer's income tax liability at 28 percent; that change would decrease deficits by a total of $0.5 trillion over the next decade.
- Other proposals in the President's budget include some initiatives that would widen the deficit and others that would narrow it. Those other proposals would change revenues and noninterest outlays by amounts that sum to a net reduction in deficits of about $0.2 trillion over the 2013–2022 period.
- Because the net revenue reductions and spending increases that would occur under the President's budget would increase deficits relative to CBO's baseline projections, the amount of interest paid on the debt would also rise. In total, net interest outlays under the President's budget would exceed the amounts projected in CBO's current-law baseline by $0.6 trillion over the 2013–2022 period.

Under current law, a number of significant changes are scheduled to occur to policies that are now in place. To provide another benchmark against which budgetary proposals can be measured—largely reflecting current policies rather than current law—CBO has also developed an alternative fiscal scenario. It incorporates the assumptions that tax provisions that have recently expired or are set to expire (other than the 2 percentage-point reduction in the payroll tax rate for Social Security) are extended through 2022, that the AMT is indexed for inflation after 2011, that Medicare's payment rates for physicians' services are held constant at their current level, and that the automatic spending reductions required by the Budget Control Act do not take effect (although the original caps on discretionary appropriations in that law are assumed to remain in place). Under that scenario, budget deficits would total $10.7 trillion over the 2013–2022 period, and debt held by the public would rise to $23.0 trillion by 2022. Deficits and debt under the President's budget, though significantly larger than in CBO's baseline, would be significantly smaller than the amounts projected in the alternative fiscal scenario (see Figures 1 and 2).[6]

CBO's estimates of deficits under the President's budget are generally smaller than those of the Administration— by $74 billion (or 6 percent) for 2012 and by a total of $294 billion (or 4 percent) for the following 10 years. CBO projects $1.5 trillion (or 3 percent) less in outlays under the President's budget than the Administration does, because of differences both in economic assumptions and in modeling and other technical assumptions. CBO's estimates of revenues under the President's budget are also lower than the Administration's—by $1.2 trillion (or 3 percent)—primarily because of differing economic assumptions (particularly about wages and salaries).

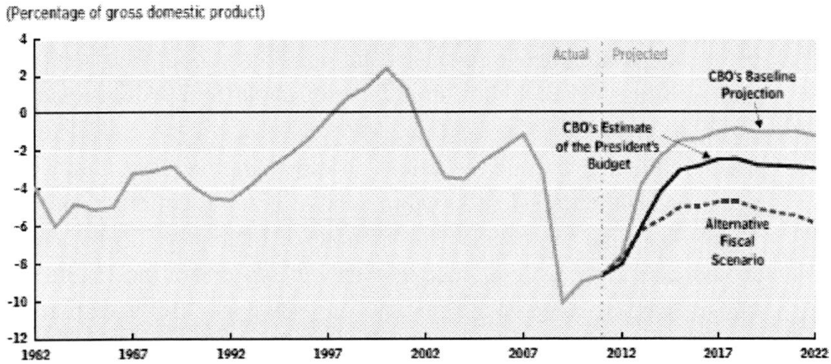

Source: Congressional Budget Office.

Note: The alternative fiscal scenario incorporates the assumptions that all expiring tax provisions (other than the payroll tax reduction), including those that expired at the end of December 2011, are instead extended; that the alternative minimum tax is indexed for inflation after 2011 (starting at the 2011 exemption amount); that Medicare's payment rates for physicians' services are held constant at their current level; and that the automatic spending reductions specified by the Budget Control Act of 2011 do not take effect.

Figure 1. Deficits Projected in CBO's Baseline, Under the President's Budget, and Under an Alternative Fiscal Scenario.

Impact of the President's Proposals on the Budget Outlook

Enacting the President's policy proposals would boost the 2012 deficit by $82 billion—to a total of $1,253 billion—relative to CBO's current-law baseline (see Table 3 on page 8). That increase would result from an additional

$20 billion in outlays in 2012 and a decrease of $61 billion in revenues. In 2013, the deficit under the President's budget would be $365 billion greater than the deficit that CBO projects in its latest baseline, because revenues would be $228 billion (or 8 percent) lower, and outlays would be $137 billion (or 4 percent) higher.[7]

Over the 2013–2022 period, the cumulative deficit that would result from enacting the President's budget— $6.4 trillion (or 3.2 percent of GDP)— would be $3.5 trillion larger than the cumulative deficit projected under current law. About $2.9 trillion of that difference stems directly from proposed policy changes, and the other $0.6 trillion reflects additional interest payments resulting from increased federal borrowing.

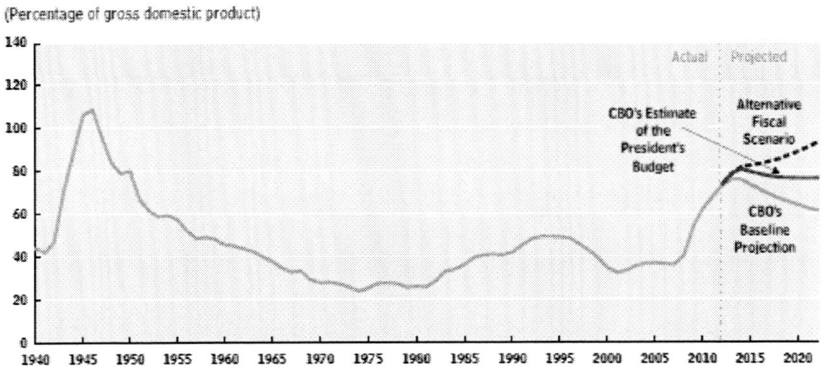

Source: Congressional Budget Office.

Note: The alternative fiscal scenario incorporates the assumptions that all expiring tax provisions (other than the payroll tax reduction), including those that expired at the end of December 2011, are instead extended; that the alternative minimum tax is indexed for inflation after 2011 (starting at the 2011 exemption amount); that Medicare's payment rates for physicians' services are held constant at their current level; and that the automatic spending reductions specified by the Budget Control Act of 2011 do not take effect.

Figure 2. Federal Debt Held by the Public Projected in CBO's Baseline, Under the President's Budget, and Under an Alternative Fiscal Scenario.

Effects on Revenues

The President is proposing to make a number of changes to tax law. If enacted, those changes would reduce revenues by $61 billion in 2012 and by $2.4 trillion—or about 6 percent—during the 2013–2022 period relative to the amounts in CBO's baseline. Those totals represent the net effect of the President's tax proposals, some of which would reduce revenues and others of which would increase them. (Those revenue proposals would also boost outlays by $442 billion between 2013 and 2022, mostly from increases in refundable tax credits and, to a lesser extent, from the spending component of a proposal to reinstate and alter the Build America Bonds program, which would raise outlays and revenues by similar amounts.) As a share of GDP, revenues would rise from 17.2 percent in 2013 to 19.8 percent in 2022 under the President's budget. Between 2015 and 2022, they would average 19.6 percent of GDP—1.2 percentage points below CBO's baseline projection but 1.7 percentage points above the average ratio of revenues to GDP seen over the past 40 years.

Extending and Modifying the 2001 and 2003 Tax Reductions

Various income tax provisions that were originally enacted in EGTRRA and JGTRRA, modified by the American Recovery and Reinvestment Act of 2009 (ARRA, P.L. 111-5), and extended by the 2010 tax act are scheduled to expire at the end of December 2012. Those provisions include reductions in some individual income tax rates, cuts in tax rates on capital gains and dividends, elimination of the phaseout of personal exemptions and the limit on itemized deductions for certain taxpayers, an increase in the child tax credit, relief from the so-called marriage penalty, and changes in the tax treatment of certain investments in equipment by small businesses.

As estimated by the staff of the Joint Committee on Taxation (JCT), the President's proposal to make those provisions permanent—with some modifications—would reduce revenues by $2.1 trillion (or 1.0 percent of GDP) over the next 10 years and increase outlays by $314 billion (or 0.2 percent of GDP) relative to the amounts in CBO's baseline.[8] (Some of those proposals would affect outlays because the tax credits involved are refundable.) Specifically, the President has called for permanently extending, at 2012 levels, the tax rates on income, capital gains, and dividends for couples with income below $250,000 who file joint tax returns and for single filers with income below $200,000. (Both of those income thresholds would be adjusted for inflation since 2009.) For taxpayers with income above the thresholds, the President proposes to maintain the income tax rates, the phaseout of the personal exemption, and the limit on itemized deductions that are scheduled to take effect in January 2013 under current law and to tax capital gains at a rate of 20 percent. In addition, the President proposes to continue the $1,000 child tax credit (which was raised by $500 in EGTRRA) and the reduced earnings threshold at which families can qualify for at least some of that credit (which was enacted in ARRA).

Providing Relief from the Alternative Minimum Tax

Besides extending those tax provisions, the President proposes to reduce the number of taxpayers who would be subject to the AMT by permanently setting various parameters of the tax at the levels that were in effect in calendar year 2011 and indexing those amounts for inflation in later years. Those parameters include the AMT exemption amount, the income threshold for phasing out that exemption amount, and the income threshold for the 28 percent tax rate. The President also proposes to make permanent the unrestricted use of certain personal tax credits under the AMT. Relative to current law, those changes would reduce revenues by $855 billion between 2013 and 2022, JCT estimates.[9]

Limiting Deductions and Exclusions

The President proposes to limit the extent to which higher-income taxpayers can reduce their tax liability through certain deductions and exclusions to 28 percent of those deductions and exclusions. The limit would apply to itemized deductions as well as to deductions or exclusions for tax-exempt interest, employer-sponsored health insurance, and employees' retirement contributions, among other things. That change would boost revenues by $523 billion over the 2013–2022 period, according to JCT.

Modifying Estate and Gift Taxes

The President's budget calls for setting the parameters of the estate, gift, and generation-skipping transfer taxes at the levels that were in effect during calendar year 2009, starting in January 2013. Under that proposal, the amount of an estate that would effectively be exempt from the estate tax would be set permanently at $3.5 million (and at $7 million per couple in most cases); any amount above that effective exemption level would be taxed at a rate of 45 percent. The exemption amount for gift taxes would be set at $1 million, with a top tax rate of 45 percent. Transfers of wealth from a decedent to an heir more than one generation younger (such as a grandchild) would also be taxed at 45 percent. Those proposals, along with some other changes to those taxes, are estimated to lower revenues by $245 billion between 2013 and 2022.

Other Revenue Proposals

Other proposals in the President's budget would reduce revenues by $48 billion this year but would increase revenues, on net, by $300 billion over the 2013–2022 period. Those proposals include a set of changes to the U.S. system of taxing international income that would raise revenues by $168 billion over 10 years, JCT estimates. The changes include targeting specific sources of tax avoidance associated with intangible assets (such as patents and trademarks) and modifying tax rules for calculating foreign tax credits and expenses related to foreign operations. The tax credit for research and experimentation expired at the end of calendar year 2011. The President proposes to permanently reinstate it, in modified form, and make it retroactive to January 1, 2012. Those changes would decrease revenues by $96 billion over the 2013–2022 period, according to JCT.

The American Opportunity Tax Credit, which was created by ARRA and extended through December 2012 by the 2010 tax act, provides an annual tax credit of up to $2,500 per student for qualifying postsecondary education expenses. The President also proposes to make that credit permanent and to index the amount of qualifying expenses and the phaseout limits for inflation. JCT estimates that those changes would decrease revenues by $81 billion over the next 10 years and increase outlays by $27 billion, thus adding $108 billion to the cumulative deficit over that period. The Build America Bonds program, which was also created by ARRA, provides subsidy payments to state and local governments that equal 35 percent of their interest costs on taxable bonds issued through December 31, 2010, to finance capital expenditures. The program has expired for bonds issued after that date; the President proposes to permanently reinstate and expand it but to lower the subsidy rate to 30 percent through 2013 and to 28 percent thereafter. By substituting taxable bonds for tax-exempt bonds, the program increases taxable interest income. According to JCT, the President's changes would raise revenues by $63 billion between 2013 and 2022. They would also boost subsidy payments to state and local governments, which are recorded in the federal budget as outlays, by an estimated $70 billion over 10 years. Thus, the net effect of those changes would be to increase the cumulative 10-year deficit by $7 billion. The President also proposes to extend through 2012 a provision that allows all firms that invest in equipment to deduct the full costs of that equipment from their taxable income immediately, instead of spreading the costs out over time. That provision would decrease revenues by $32 billion in 2012 but boost them by $27 billion over the 2013–2022 period, JCT estimates.

Taken together, all of the remaining revenue proposals in the President's budget would raise revenues by $219 billion over the next 10 years relative to current law. Proposals that CBO and JCT estimate would increase revenues include repealing the "last-in, first-out" method of accounting for inventories (an increase of $67 billion between 2013 and 2022); imposing a "financial crisis responsibility fee" ($61 billion);[10] providing short-term tax relief to employers and expanding the base for the payroll tax for unemployment compensation ($30 billion); and boosting spending for enforcement activities of the Internal Revenue Service ($35 billion).[11] Partly offsetting those revenue increases would be revenue reductions from extending through 2013 a host of tax provisions that have been extended in past years ($41 billion).

Effects on Outlays

On the spending side of the budget, the President's policies would increase noninterest outlays by $19 billion in 2012 and by $564 billion (or 1 percent) between 2013 and 2022 relative to CBO's baseline projections. Because the President's revenue and spending proposals together would increase deficits and thus require additional federal borrowing, they would also raise interest costs—by an estimated $586 billion over the 2013–2022 period. Total outlays would equal 23.4 percent of GDP in 2013, decline as a share of GDP through 2018, and then rise. They would equal 22.8 percent of GDP in 2022— about 0.4 percentage points higher than CBO's baseline projection for that year and well above the 21.0 percent average seen over the past 40 years.

Excluding interest costs, total outlays would exceed the amounts in CBO's baseline in each year from 2012 to 2021. However, such outlays would be lower than CBO's baseline projection in 2022 as a result of a shift in the timing of certain payments for benefit programs. (Under current law, those payments will move into fiscal year 2022 from 2023 because the normal payment date, October 1, falls on a weekend. The President proposes to shift the payments back into fiscal year 2023.)

Outlays for mandatory programs would be $1.2 trillion higher through 2022 under the President's budget than in CBO's baseline, largely because of two factors: a reclassification of spending for surface transportation that is currently categorized as discretionary, and a greater amount of refundable tax credits. Relative to GDP, mandatory outlays would equal 14.0 percent in 2013 under the President's budget and generally remain at or above that level; by 2022, mandatory outlays would equal 14.6 percent of GDP, 0.2 percentage points higher than in CBO's baseline. For discretionary programs, the President's budget reflects spending over the next 10 years that is nearly $600 billion below the amounts in CBO's baseline, mainly because less funding is proposed for war-related activities than is projected in the baseline and because transportation spending is reclassified. In total, discretionary outlays would drop from 7.9 percent of GDP in 2013 to 5.2 percent in 2022, 0.4 percentage points lower than in CBO's baseline.

Table 3. CBO's Estimate of the Effect of the President's Budget on Baseline Deficits (Billions of dollars)

												Total	
												2013-	*2013-*
	2012	*2013*	*2014*	*2015*	*2016*	*2017*	*2018*	*2019*	*2020*	*2021*	*2022*	*2017*	*2022*
Deficit in CBO's March 2012 Baseline	-1,171	-612	-385	-257	-259	-201	-175	-224	-234	-237	-303	-1,713	-2,887
Effect of the President's Proposals													
Revenues													
Provisions related to EGTRRA and JGTRRA[a]													
Modify individual income tax rates[b]	0	-75	-109	-116	-124	-132	-140	-149	-157	-165	-174	-555	-1,341
Provide relief from the marriage penalty	0	-20	-30	-32	-35	-37	-39	-41	-43	-45	-47	-154	-370
Extend child tax credit provisions[c]	0	-3	-13	-13	-14	-14	-14	-14	-14	-14	-14	-57	-129
Modify tax rates on capital gains and dividends[d]	-1	-5	-8	-15	-15	-15	-15	-15	-16	-16	-17	-58	-137
Other provisions	*	-6	-12	-11	-11	-11	-10	-10	-10	-10	-11	-50	-101
Subtotal	-1	-108	-173	-187	-198	-208	-219	-230	-241	-252	-262	-874	-2,077
Index the AMT starting from 2011 levels[a]	-9	-94	-42	-49	-57	-66	-78	-92	-107	-125	-144	-308	-855
Limit the tax rate at which deductions and exclusions													
reduce tax liability	-3	19	43	43	48	52	56	60	64	67	71	205	523
Modify estate and gift tax provisions	*	-1	-19	-22	-24	-26	-27	-29	-31	-32	-34	-91	-245
Modify the U.S. international tax system	0	7	15	16	17	18	19	19	20	19	18	73	168
Extend the research and experimentation tax credit	-3	-5	-6	-7	-8	-9	-10	-11	-12	-13	-14	-36	-96
Extend the American Opportunity Credit	0	-2	-7	-8	-8	-8	-9	-9	-9	-10	-10	-34	-81
Reinstate and modify the Build America													
Bonds program[e]	*	1	2	3	4	5	7	8	10	11	13	14	63
Extend full expensing for certain property	-32	-16	13	9	7	6	3	2	1	1	1	19	27
Other proposals	-13	-28	-3	25	38	39	30	26	32	31	29	71	219
Total Effect on Revenues	*-61*	*-228*	*-178*	*-176*	*-181*	*-198*	*-229*	*-256*	*-274*	*-301*	*-333*	*-961*	*-2,354*

												Total	
												2013-2017	2013-2022
	2012	2013	2014	2015	2016	2017	2018	2019	2020	2021	2022		
Outlays													
Mandatory													
Reclassify surface transportation spending as mandatory	0	15	35	45	49	53	55	57	58	59	61	196	486
Other changes to transportation programs	*	10	13	11	13	16	20	17	10	6	4	65	123
Extend or expand certain refundable tax credits	*	1	39	39	40	41	41	41	41	42	42	160	366
Freeze Medicare's physician payment rates at 2012 level	0	11	18	21	24	26	28	31	34	37	41	100	271
Other changes to Medicare	*	*	-8	-18	-22	-26	-30	-32	-39	-46	-54	-74	-276
Changes to Medicaid	0	1	2	-3	-4	-9	-9	-10	-9	-10	-15	-14	-66
Reinstate and modify the Build America													
Bonds program[e]	*	1	2	3	4	6	7	9	11	12	14	16	70
Eliminate automatic spending reductions[f]	0	9	13	13	14	14	15	16	17	17	6	64	134
Other proposals	18	45	29	23	7	2	-1	-1	-2	-2	-45	106	54
Subtotal	19	93	144	136	124	122	127	128	120	116	53	619	1,163
Outlays (Continued)													
Discretionary													
Eliminate automatic spending reductions[f]	0	56	79	87	89	91	90	89	88	87	88	402	845
Changes to spending on overseas contingency operationsg	0	-12	-52	-75	-85	-90	-93	-96	-99	-102	-106	-313	-810
Reclassify surface transportation spending as mandatory	0	-15	-35	-45	-49	-53	-55	-57	-58	-59	-61	-196	-486
Other	*	11	-4	-12	-17	-23	-22	-21	-19	-21	-21	-44	-148
Subtotal	*	41	-12	-44	-62	-75	-80	-85	-88	-95	-100	-151	-598
Net interest	2	4	7	14	27	42	59	78	98	119	139	93	586
Total Effect on Outlays	20	137	139	106	90	89	106	121	131	139	92	561	1,150

Table 3. (Continued)

(Billions of dollars)													
												Total	
												2013-	*2013-*
	2012	*2013*	*2014*	*2015*	*2016*	*2017*	*2018*	*2019*	*2020*	*2021*	*2022*	*2017*	*2022*
Total Effect on the Deficith	-82	-365	-317	-282	-270	-287	-335	-377	-404	-440	-425	-1,522	-3,504
Deficit Under the President's Budget as Estimated by CBO	-1,253	-977	-702	-539	-529	-488	-510	-602	-638	-678	-728	-3,235	-6,390
Memorandum:													
Total Effects of Eliminating Automatic Spending Reductionsf	0	65	92	101	103	105	105	105	105	104	94	466	980

Sources: Congressional Budget Office; Staff of the Joint Committee on Taxation.

Note: EGTRRA = Economic Growth and Tax Relief Reconciliation Act of 2001; JGTRRA = Jobs and Growth Tax Relief Reconciliation Act of 2003; AMT = alternative minimum tax; * = between -$500 million and $500 million.

[a] The estimated effects of the President's proposals related to EGTRRA and JGTRRA interact with the effects of the proposal to index the AMT. This analysis first estimated the revenue effects of the proposal for the AMT relative to projections under current law, and then it estimated the effects of the proposals related to EGTRRA and JGTRRA relative to projections under current law modified for the proposed changes to the AMT. Thus, the estimates for the proposals related to EGTRRA and JGTRRA include estimated losses in revenues that would result from interactions with the AMT proposal.

[b] The estimates include the effects of maintaining, for taxpayers with income above certain levels, the income tax rates of 36 percent and 39.6 percent scheduled to go into effect in calendar year 2013 under current law. For other taxpayers, tax rates would be at the levels originally specified in EGTRRA and extended through calendar year 2012 in the Tax Relief, Unemployment Insurance Reauthorization, and Job Creation Act of 2010.

[c] This proposal includes extending the $1,000 child tax credit and the use of that credit to reduce AMT liability.

[d] The estimate includes the effect of maintaining the capital gains and dividend tax rates of zero and 15 percent for couples who file joint tax returns and have income below $250,000 and for single filers who have income below $200,000.

[e] This proposal affects revenues and outlays. The staff of the Joint Committee on Taxation estimates that the net effect of the proposal for the Build America Bonds program is to increase the deficit by $7 billion over the 2013–2022 period.

[f] The Budget Control Act specified that if legislation originating with the Joint Select Committee on Deficit Reduction to reduce the deficit was not enacted, automatic procedures to cut both discretionary and mandatory spending during the coming decade would take effect. Because the committee did not report any legislation, those reductions are scheduled to go into effect on January 2, 2013. The President's budget does not include such automatic spending reductions.

[g] These changes reflect the net effect of replacing the baseline extrapolation of funding for overseas contingency operations with the President's request for such funding.

[h] Negative numbers indicate an increase in the deficit relative to CBO's baseline.

Proposals That Would Affect Mandatory Spending

The proposal with the largest impact on mandatory spending is the one to reclassify most funding for surface transportation programs from discretionary to mandatory (including all surface transportation programs funded through the Highway Trust Fund). That reclassification would not, by itself, have any net budgetary impact, but it would boost mandatory outlays (and reduce discretionary outlays) by $486 billion over the 2013–2022 period.[12] All other changes to transportation programs proposed by the President would increase mandatory outlays, on net, by $123 billion over the next 10 years.

The President proposes to extend or expand various refundable tax credits, including the earned income tax credit, the child tax credit, and some education credits. Other tax proposals in the President's budget, particularly the extension of certain provisions originally enacted in EGTRRA and JGTRRA, would also affect the refundable portion of tax credits. All told, the President's policy changes would increase outlays for refundable credits by an estimated $366 billion over the 2013–2022 period.

Under current law, Medicare's payment rates for physicians' services are slated to drop by 27 percent in January 2013 and by additional amounts in later years. The President proposes to avoid those reductions by freezing payment rates at their 2012 level for the next 10 years. That freeze would increase net outlays by $271 billion over the 2013–2022 period, CBO estimates.

The President's budget includes numerous other proposals involving Medicare, most of which are designed to reduce the program's spending. Several provisions would modify payments to health care providers, such as hospitals and skilled nursing facilities. In addition, the President proposes to modify cost-sharing responsibilities for some Medicare beneficiaries. Additional savings would result from proposals to require manufacturers to pay rebates on drugs dispensed to low-income beneficiaries enrolled in Part D of Medicare and to reduce payment rates for certain biological drugs (products derived from living material) covered under Part B of the program. Finally, the budget includes several provisions designed to reduce waste, fraud, and abuse in Medicare. In all, those policies (other than the freeze on physicians' payment rates) would reduce Medicare outlays by $276 billion over 10 years, CBO estimates.[13]

The President is also seeking a number of changes to the Medicaid program, which, if adopted, would generate net savings of $66 billion over the 2013–2022 period relative to CBO's baseline. The President proposes to limit the amount of revenues from taxes on health care providers that states can use to pay their portion of Medicaid costs, beginning in 2015. In addition, under current law, states receive different federal matching rates for expenditures under Medicaid and the Children's Health Insurance Program (CHIP), and they will receive enhanced matching rates beginning in 2014 for people who become eligible for Medicaid as a result of the Affordable Care Act.[14] The President proposes to replace that rate structure, starting in 2017, with a single matching rate for each state; that rate would automatically increase if a recession forced enrollment and states' costs to rise. Other proposed changes to Medicaid include limiting certain payment rates and, in 2022, limiting reimbursements for hospitals that serve a disproportionate number of poor and uninsured people.

The proposal discussed above to reinstate and expand the Build America Bonds program and lower its subsidy rate would boost outlays by $70 billion through 2022, JCT estimates. Combined with the corresponding revenue increase of $63 billion, that proposal would result in a net increase of $7 billion in the cumulative 10-year deficit.

In addition, the automatic enforcement procedures specified by the Budget Control Act are set to go into effect in January 2013 and to reduce mandatory spending by an estimated $134 billion over the next 10 years. The President's budget does not include those reductions, thereby boosting mandatory outlays relative to the current-law baseline.

All of the other proposed changes to mandatory programs, taken together, would increase outlays by $18 billion in 2012 and by $54 billion over the 2013– 2022 period. Such changes include the President's proposals to significantly increase funding in 2012 for certain education and job-training activities, such as subsidizing summer employment for young people and providing grants to states to pay teachers and modernize schools. Those proposals, which are similar to ones made by the Administration last fall, would increase spending by $11 billion in 2012 and by $69 billion over the 2013– 2022 period, CBO estimates.

Proposals That Would Affect Discretionary Spending

For 2012, discretionary budget authority would be slightly greater under the President's budget than in CBO's baseline.[15] The only difference is that the President is requesting supplemental funding of $0.4 billion for additional program-integrity initiatives aimed at reducing wasteful or fraudulent spending in certain entitlement programs.

For 2013, the President has requested $1.15 trillion in discretionary budget authority, which is $52 billion (or 4 percent) less than the amount enacted for 2012 plus the request for supplemental funding (see Table 4). More than half of the reduction between those two years ($30 billion) would result from decreased appropriations for overseas contingency operations; other appropriations would decline by about 2 percent. In 2014, total discretionary funding under the President's budget would drop by 4 percent, to $1.1 trillion, but it would grow in later years, reaching $1.3 trillion in 2022.

Most appropriations for 2013 through 2021 are constrained by caps put in place by the Budget Control Act (although funding for certain purposes, such as OCO, is not limited by those caps).[16] The caps currently in law apply separately to defense and nondefense budget authority for each year, but the President's budget refers to a classification in the Budget Control Act that was previously in effect and that applies caps to "security" and "nonsecurity" funding for 2013 and to a single discretionary category from 2014 to 2021.[17] By CBO's estimate, the total appropriations requested for 2013 that are constrained by the caps are roughly equal to the total amount of the caps for that year ($1,043 billion, which represents the $1,047 billion specified in current law, adjusted downward by about $4 billion to account for the President's proposal to reclassify some surface transportation programs as mandatory). However, according to CBO's estimates, appropriations for 2013 in the security category would exceed their cap by $2 billion, whereas nonsecurity appropriations would fall below their cap by about the same amount (after adjusting for the reclassification proposal).[18] Nevertheless, by the Administration's estimate—which is the one that would determine whether a sequestration (an automatic cancellation of budgetary resources) would go into effect—no breach of either cap would take place.

On top of the $1,043 billion in proposed budget authority for 2013 that is limited by the caps, the President proposes $104 billion in funding for that year that would- not be constrained by the caps. The additional funding—which, by law, the caps can be adjusted to accommodate—would be used for the following purposes:

- $97 billion for overseas contingency operations,
- $6 billion for disaster relief, and
- $2 billion for program-integrity initiatives.

Overall, budget authority for defense discretionary programs would decrease by $29 billion (or 4 percent) between 2012 and 2013 under the President's budget. Funding for defense activities classified as OCO would fall by $27 billion (or 23 percent) to $88 billion in 2013, and appropriations for other defense activities would decline by $2 billion (or 0.4 percent).

Table 4. Proposed Changes in Discretionary Budget Authority in the President's Budget, 2011 to 2013 (Billions of dollars)

	Actual, 2011	*Administration's Request*		*Percentage Change*	
		2012[a]	*2013*	*2011–2012*	*2012–2013*
Defense					
Overseas contingency operations[b]	159	115	88	-27.6	-23.3
Other	551	554	552	0.5	-0.4
Subtotal	711	670	640	-5.8	-4.4
Nondefense					
Overseas contingency operations[b]	0	11	8	n.a.	-26.4
Other	510	518	498	1.5	-3.8
Subtotal	510	529	507	3.7	-4.3
Total	*1,221*	*1,199*	*1,147*	*-1.8*	*-4.3*

Source: Congressional Budget Office.

Notes: The numbers shown here do not include obligation limitations for certain transportation programs. n.a. = not applicable.

[a] The Administration's request for discretionary b7udget authority for 2012 reflects the appropriations enacted for this year plus $410 million for additional program-integrity initiatives aimed at reducing wasteful or fraudulent spending in certain entitlement programs.

[b] In this table, "overseas contingency operations" refers to military operations in Iraq and Afghanistan and related activities.

For nondefense discretionary programs, budget authority would decrease by $23 billion (or 4 percent) between 2012 and 2013 under the President's budget. That drop stems mainly from four sources:

- A shift of $8 billion for the Department of Justice's Crime Victims Fund from 2013 into 2014,
- A proposal to reduce by $6.7 billion the funding available for paying performance bonuses to states under CHIP in 2013,[19]
- An additional $5 billion in receipts that CBO expects the Federal Housing Administration to receive in 2013 under current law because of increases in the volume of loans and in premiums (relative to 2012) for the mortgage guarantees that it provides, and

- A reduction in budget authority of $4.2 billion in 2013 because of the proposal to reclassify many surface transportation programs from discretionary to mandatory.[20]

Under the President's budget, most other nondefense discretionary programs would receive funding for 2013 similar to what was provided for 2012.

Thereafter, total discretionary budget authority proposed by the President would rise by an average of about 2 percent per year—from $1.1 trillion in 2014 to $1.3 trillion in 2022. The proposed funding includes a placeholder of $44 billion a year for OCO (although the Administration does not specify how much of that future request would be classified as defense spending).[21] The totals do not include any further request for disaster relief funding, but they include requests of between $2 billion and $4 billion a year for program-integrity initiatives. Between 2014 and 2021, appropriations subject to the overall cap on discretionary spending in the President's budget would be below that cap in each year (after adjusting for the proposal to reclassify some surface transportation programs as mandatory).

Outlays from the discretionary budget authority requested in the President's budget would total $1.26 trillion in 2013 and then decline to $1.15 trillion in 2015 before beginning to grow again. Such outlays would reach $1.28 trillion in 2022, returning to about the same level anticipated for 2013. As a share of GDP, discretionary outlays would fall from 9.0 percent in 2011 to 5.2 percent in 2022—the lowest level in the past 50 years. Cumulative outlays over the 2013–2022 period would be nearly $600 billion (or 5 percent) less than CBO's baseline projection, largely because OCO funding would be set below the level assumed in the baseline and because spending for most surface transportation programs would be reclassified as mandatory, thereby reducing discretionary outlays between 2013 and 2022 by $810 billion and $486 billion, respectively. Such reductions would be partially offset by eliminating the automatic spending cuts (which would increase discretionary outlays by $845 billion) currently scheduled for 2013 through 2021. Other proposed changes to discretionary programs would reduce outlays by $148 billion during the 2013– 2022 period.

Effect of the President's Proposals on Net Interest

The policy changes in the President's budget would increase the government's borrowing needs by $3.6 trillion over the 2013–2022 period (including the effect on nonbudgetary cash flows for credit programs); as a result, outlays for net interest payments would exceed the amounts projected in CBO's baseline by nearly $590 billion over that period. In nominal dollars (without adjusting for inflation), net interest costs would triple during those 10 years: from $237 billion in 2013 to $743 billion in 2022. Relative to the size of the economy, net interest payments would amount to 3.0 percent of GDP in 2022 under the President's budget, about 0.6 percentage points higher than in the baseline and double the percentage estimated for 2013.

Differences Between CBO's and the Administration's Estimates of the President's Budget

On net, CBO's estimate of the cumulative deficit for the 2013–2022 period that would result under the President's budget is about 5 percent less than the Administration's estimate. However, there are significant differences, mostly offsetting, in projections of revenues and outlays.

For 2012, CBO's estimate of the deficit under the President's budget is $74 billion smaller than the shortfall estimated by the Administration; the difference stems from a $148 billion lower estimate of outlays, which is partly offset by a lower estimate of revenues. For the following 10 years, CBO's estimate of the cumulative deficit under the President's budget is about $300 billion below the Administration's estimate, because CBO's projections of outlays are $1.5 trillion lower and its projections of revenues are $1.2 trillion lower (see Table 5).

Differences in Estimates of Revenues

CBO attributes the bulk of the difference in revenue estimates for 2012 to differences in the outlook for the economy. In particular, CBO projects lower amounts of personal income, especially wages and salaries, and of corporate profits.

For the 2013–2022 period, CBO projects 3 percent less in revenues under the President's proposals than the Administration does. That disparity results almost entirely from different baseline projections rather than from different assessments of the impact of the President's proposals. CBO's baseline projections of revenues over that period are about $1.6 trillion lower than the Administration's because of different economic projections, by CBO's reckoning, but are about $0.4 trillion higher than the Administration's because of different estimates of the amount of revenue that will result from a given set of economic conditions. Specifically, CBO's economic projections imply less revenue than the Administration's do largely because CBO projects that wages and salaries—the most significant component of the tax bases for individual income and payroll taxes—will be about $3.2 trillion (or 3 percent) lower over the next 10 calendar years than the Administration projects. In addition, CBO projects that domestic economic profits—the main component of the tax base for corporate income taxes—will be $1.5 trillion (or 8 percent) lower than the Administration projects.

Differences in Estimates of Outlays

CBO's estimate of outlays in 2012 under the President's budget is $148 billion lower than the Administration's estimate, mainly because of technical differences. The proposal to reclassify some surface transportation programs affects how those technical differences are ascribed to mandatory and discretionary outlays. The President's budget reflects the assumption that the reclassification will occur this year and thus shows such outlays as mandatory in 2012. CBO, by contrast, assumes that if the policy was enacted, it would not take effect until 2013. That discrepancy is offset on the discretionary side of the ledger. Without the reclassification, the technical differences in mandatory outlays for 2012 shown in Table 5 would be -$77 billion (rather than -$129 billion), and the differences in discretionary outlays would be -$68 billion (rather than -$16 billion). On the mandatory side, CBO estimates $19 billion less in outlays for the Deposit Insurance Fund in 2012 than the Administration does, mainly because of considerably lower projections of losses. Another large difference for 2012 results from differing estimates for a policy proposal: CBO estimates that certain increases in education funding proposed by the President would be spent more slowly than the Administration expects, leading to a $20 billion lower estimate of outlays for this year. On the discretionary side, CBO's estimates of defense spending in 2012 are $36 billion below the Administration's, primarily because of differences in estimates for military procurement ($14 billion lower), operations and maintenance ($13 billion lower), and research and development ($6 billion lower). In addition, CBO estimates about $4 billion less in outlays this year for loans to manufacturers of energy-efficient vehicles and related components and about $3 billion less in spending on disaster relief.

Table 5. Sources of Differences Between CBO's and the Administration's Estimates of the President's Budget (Billions of dollars)

												Total	
												2013-2017	2013-2022
	2012	2013	2014	2015	2016	2017	2018	2019	2020	2021	2022		
				Administration's Estimate									
Deficit Under the President's Budget	-1,327	-901	-668	-610	-649	-612	-575	-626	-658	-681	-704	-3,440	-6,684
		Differences Between CBO's and the Administration's Estimates											
Differences in Revenues[a]													
Economic	-87	-166	-155	-122	-108	-140	-171	-188	-193	-185	-175	-691	-1,604
Technical	13	5	44	84	85	89	61	37	34	-10	-56	308	373
Total	-74	-161	-111	-37	-23	-51	-110	-151	-159	-195	-231	-384	-1,230
Differences in Outlays[b]													
Mandatory													
Economic	-4	-6	-7	-16	-27	-32	-34	-38	-41	-45	-51	-88	-298
Technical	-129	-66	-38	-22	-18	-18	-11	-15	-20	-37	-44	-162	-289
Subtotal	-133	-73	-45	-38	-45	-49	-45	-53	-62	-82	-95	-250	-587
Discretionary (Technical)	-16	-2	23	20	15	-3	-13	-11	-11	-10	-5	52	3
Net interest													
Economic	-4	-20	-55	-87	-103	-101	-86	-69	-56	-47	-41	-367	-664
Technical	4	9	1	-3	-10	-22	-33	-43	-50	-59	-66	-25	-276
Subtotal	1	-11	-54	-90	-113	-123	-118	-111	-106	-106	-107	-392	-940
Total	-148	-86	-76	-108	-143	-175	-176	-175	-179	-198	-207	-589	-1,524
Total Differencesa	74	-75	-34	71	120	124	66	24	20	3	-24	205	294

Table 5. (Continued)

												Total	
												2013-	2013-
	2012	2013	2014	2015	2016	2017	2018	2019	2020	2021	2022	2017	2022
				CBO's Estimate									
Deficit Under the President's Budget	-1,253	-977	-702	-539	-529	-488	-510	-602	-638	-678	-728	-3,235	-6,390
Memorandum:													
Total Economic Differencesa	-80	-139	-93	-19	22	-8	-51	-82	-96	-93	-83	-237	-641
Total Technical Differencesa	153	64	58	90	98	132	116	106	115	96	59	442	935

Sources: Congressional Budget Office; Staff of the Joint Committee on Taxation.

[a] Positive numbers indicate that such differences cause CBO's estimate of the deficit to be lower than the Administration's estimate.

[b] Positive numbers indicate that such differences cause CBO's estimate of the deficit to be higher than the Administration's estimate.

For the 2013–2022 period, CBO's projection of total outlays under the President's budget is $1.5 trillion below that of the Administration, almost entirely because of a nearly $600 billion (or 2 percent) difference in estimates of mandatory spending and a $940 billion (or 16 percent) difference in estimates of net interest.

The total difference over 10 years between CBO's and the Administration's estimates of mandatory spending under the President's budget is nearly evenly attributable to economic differences ($298 billion) and technical factors ($289 billion). Differing projections of Social Security outlays account for $186 billion of the economic differences; compared with the Administration, CBO projects lower cost-of-living adjustments in most of the next 10 years (an average of 0.4 percentage points lower per year through 2017) and lower average wages for Social Security participants (which lead to lower initial benefit levels). In addition, CBO's projections of Medicare outlays are nearly $84 billion lower than the Administration's for economic reasons, mainly because of lower projections for the indexes used to calculate prices for Medicare providers.

CBO's estimates of mandatory spending in the 2013– 2022 period under the President's budget are $289 billion lower than the Administration's for technical reasons because of differences in baselines as well as different estimates of the President's policy proposals. The largest technical differences involve estimates of outlays for veterans' compensation and pensions, for Fannie Mae and Freddie Mac, and for Medicaid, as well as the reclassification of surface transportation programs. The Administration projects much higher growth in the population of veterans receiving disability compensation over the next 10 years and higher average benefit payments. As a result, CBO's baseline projection of outlays for veterans' compensation is $235 billion lower than the Administration's for that period. Conversely, CBO's baseline projection of costs related to Fannie Mae and Freddie Mac is nearly $210 billion higher than that of the Administration, mostly because CBO's total is in accord with the budgetary practices used for federal credit programs and reflects the anticipated subsidy cost (including an adjustment for market risk) of mortgage guarantees issued by Fannie Mae and Freddie Mac. The Administration, by contrast, records the net payments to and receipts from those two entities.[22] The divergence in baseline projections for Medicaid results from differing estimates of enrollment and other factors; such differences cause CBO's baseline projection to exceed the Administration's by $157 billion over the 2013–2022 period. Technical differences in estimates of mandatory spending are also affected by differing classifications of some surface transportation funding provided before 2013. As noted above, CBO's estimate of the President's budget reflects the assumption that the reclassification would not occur until 2013 and that future outlays from funding provided before that year would remain classified as discretionary; the Administration considers such outlays in 2012 and beyond as mandatory, regardless of when the original funding was provided. That difference in classification is largely responsible for CBO's $131 billion lower estimate of mandatory outlays for surface transportation between 2013 and 2022; the difference has the opposite effect on estimates of discretionary spending.

CBO's estimates of discretionary outlays under the President's budget are significantly lower than the Administration's for a number of programs. The largest such differences involve the Pell Grant program ($58 billion) and mortgage credit programs administered by the Federal Housing Administration ($20 billion).

CBO's estimates of net interest outlays under the President's budget are lower than the Administration's by $940 billion over the 2013–2022 period. About 70 percent of that difference ($664 billion) is economic in nature and occurs primarily because CBO projects lower interest rates for the coming decade than the Administration does. On average for that period, CBO anticipates rates that are 0.6 percentage points lower for 3-month Treasury bills and 0.5 percentage points lower for 10-year Treasury notes. The other 30 percent of the difference in projections of net interest ($276 billion) stems mainly from differences in assumptions about the mix of securities that the Treasury will issue over the next 10 years.

End Notes

[1] For more details about the President's revenue proposals, see Joint Committee on Taxation, *Estimated Budget Effects of the Revenue Provisions Contained in the President's Fiscal Year 2013 Budget Proposal,* JCX-27-12 (March 14, 2012).

[2] For information about CBO's latest baseline, see Congressional Budget Office, *Updated Budget Projections: Fiscal Years 2012 to 2022* (March 2012).

[3] This analysis does not include an assessment of the macroeconomic effects of the President's proposals or the feedback from those effects on the federal budget. CBO will publish a separate analysis of those economic effects and indirect budgetary effects in a few weeks.

[4] A tax credit is refundable if the taxpayer receives a refund when the allowable credit exceeds the amount of tax owed. Such refunds are recorded in the budget as outlays.

[5] Under the provisions of that law, because the Joint Select Committee on Deficit Reduction did not report legislation to reduce the deficit, automatic procedures to cut both discretionary and mandatory spending during the coming decade are scheduled to take effect. For more

details about those procedures, see Congressional Budget Office, *The Budget and Economic Outlook: Fiscal Years 2012 to 2022* (January 2012), Box 1-2, pp. 12–13.

[6] Year-by-year data for the alternative fiscal scenario are presented in Congressional Budget Office, *Updated Budget Projections: Fiscal Years 2012 to 2022* (March 2012).

[7] Since the release of the President's budget on February 13, 2012, a number of policies have been enacted into law—most notably, an extension through December 2012 of the reduced Social Security payroll tax rate for employees—that were either proposed in the budget or were similar to proposals in the budget. CBO has incorporated the effects of all enacted legislation into its new baseline and thus does not assign any effects from those proposals to the President's budget.

[8] That revenue estimate incorporates the effects of interactions between those provisions and the President's AMT proposal discussed below. Such interactions increase the projected revenue reduction relative to what it would be without the AMT proposal.

[9] That estimate does not reflect the interactions between the AMT provisions and the proposal to extend and modify the 2001 and 2003 tax reductions extended in the 2010 tax act. The effects of those interactions are included in the estimate for that latter proposal.

[10] The Administration did not provide enough detail about the President's proposal to impose a financial crisis responsibility fee to allow for a full assessment of its effects on revenues. Additional specifications would be required for JCT to produce a revenue estimate. However, CBO incorporated the Administration's estimate (rounded to the nearest billion dollars) as a placeholder because CBO judged that the revenues estimated in the budget proposal could feasibly be raised in the general manner described.

[11] That proposal would provide funding for the Internal Revenue Service's enforcement activities above the amounts projected in CBO's baseline. If lawmakers provided such increased funding, CBO and JCT estimate that additional revenues would result, and an estimate of such revenues is included in this analysis. However, budgetary savings (such as increased revenues) from providing additional appropriations for administrative spending cannot be counted as an offset to such spending for Congressional score-keeping purposes.

[12] For programs funded through the Highway Trust Fund, budget authority is classified as mandatory under current law, but outlays are considered discretionary because they have historically been controlled by obligation limitations set in appropriation acts. Reclassifying those programs—which could be done without legislation if agreed to by the House and Senate Budget Committees, the Administration, and CBO—would shift $401 billion from the discretionary to the mandatory category over the 2013–2022 period in CBO's baseline. However, some surface transportation programs are currently funded through discretionary budget authority and would require legislation to reclassify; in CBO's baseline, outlays for those programs total $85 billion between 2013 and 2022.

[13] That figure does not include the effect on Medicare spending of the President's proposal to eliminate automatic budget enforcement procedures, which is discussed separately. CBO's March 2012 baseline projections for Medicare incorporate $88 billion in net savings from automatic procedures that would reduce payment rates for most Medicare services by 2 percent between February 2013 and January 2022.

[14] The Affordable Care Act comprises the Patient Protection and Affordable Care Act (P.L. 111-148) and the health care provisions of the Health Care and Education Reconciliation Act of 2010 (P.L. 111-152).

[15] Discretionary budget authority is the authority provided in appropriation acts to incur financial obligations that will result in immediate or future outlays.

[16] The caps discussed here do not include the further reductions called for under current law as a result of the automatic enforcement procedures in the Budget Control Act. For more details about those procedures, see Congressional Budget Office, *The Budget and Economic Outlook: Fiscal Years 2012 to 2022* (January 2012), Box 1-2, pp. 12–13.

[17] "Defense" discretionary programs are those in budget function 050; "nondefense" programs comprise all other discretionary appropriations. Under the Administration's classification (namely, the categories originally specified in the Budget Control Act), the security category would comprise discretionary appropriations for the Department of Defense, the Department of Homeland Security, the Department of Veterans Affairs, the National Nuclear Security Administration, the intelligence community management account (95-0401-0-1-054), and discretionary accounts in budget function 150 (international affairs). The nonsecurity category would comprise all other discretionary appropriations. The Budget Control Act initially set caps on discretionary appropriations using the "security" and "nonsecurity" categories. However, under the provisions of that law, because the Joint Select Committee on Deficit Reduction did not report legislation to reduce the deficit, the caps were reset to cover defense and nondefense programs to serve as the basis for the automatic spending reductions that are set to take effect in January 2013.

[18] A number of differences exist between CBO's estimates of discretionary budget authority for 2013 and the Administration's estimates. The two largest differences involve the Federal Housing Administration (FHA) and the Department of Defense. CBO estimates that more mortgages will be guaranteed by the FHA than the Administration does; those guarantees will result in more receipts to the FHA in 2013. In addition, CBO estimates that the Administration's proposal to reduce the amount of annual contributions to the Medicare-Eligible Retiree Health Care Fund would not be implemented in time to affect the 2013 accrual payments.

[19] States qualify for performance bonus payments under CHIP on an annual basis if they adopt at least five of eight specific enrollment processes (which are generally aimed at simplifying Medicaid and CHIP enrollment and renewal for children) and if the number of children enrolled in Medicaid in the state exceeds certain benchmarks. Because the President is requesting this funding change for a mandatory program through the appropriation process, it is classified as a reduction in discretionary funding. CBO does not expect the reduction to have any effect on outlays, because the amounts available for performance bonus payments, even after the proposed reduction, are well above the amounts that states are expected to qualify for.

[20] Most surface transportation programs are currently funded through mandatory budget authority provided in authorizing legislation. However, annual appropriation acts control spending for those programs by limiting how much of the budget authority the Department of Transportation can obligate.

[21] In 2012 and most previous years, some OCO funding was provided for diplomatic operations and foreign aid, which are classified as nondefense spending.

[22] The Administration treats Fannie Mae and Freddie Mac as nongovernmental organizations and records payments between them and the Treasury on a cash basis. In contrast, CBO projects the budgetary impact of Fannie Mae's and Freddie Mac's operations as if they were being conducted by a federal agency, because of the degree of management and financial control that the government exercises over the two entities. Therefore, CBO estimates the net lifetime costs—that is, the subsidy costs—of new loans and guarantees to be issued by the entities and counts those costs as federal outlays in the year of issuance. See Congressional Budget Office, *CBO's Budgetary Treatment of Fannie Mae and Freddie Mac* (January

2010), and *Fannie Mae, Freddie Mac, and the Federal Role in the Secondary Mortgage Market* (December 2010).

In: The Federal Budget: 2013 and Beyond ISBN: 978-1-62081-920-3
Editors: J. Lambert and I. Johnson

Chapter 6

THE FEDERAL GOVERNMENT'S LONG-TERM FISCAL OUTLOOK: SPRING 2012 UPDATE*

The United States Government Accountability Office

GAO'S LONG-TERM FISCAL SIMULATIONS

Since 1992, GAO has published long-term fiscal simulations showing federal deficits and debt under different sets of policy assumptions. GAO developed its long-term model in response to a bipartisan request from members of Congress concerned about the long-term effects of fiscal policy. GAO's simulations provide context for consideration of policy options. They are not intended to suggest particular policy choices or to predict the economic impact of any set of choices but to help facilitate a dialogue on this important issue.

GAO regularly updates its simulations as new data become available from the Congressional Budget Office (CBO) and the Social Security and Medicare Trustees (Trustees). This update incorporates CBO's January 2012 budget and economic projections. As in the past, GAO shows two simulations:

The *Baseline Extended* simulation follows CBO's January 2012 baseline, which generally reflects current law, for the first 10 years. The baseline

---

* This is an edited, reformatted and augmented version of The United States Government Accountability Office publication GAO-12-521SP.

includes the effects from the discretionary spending caps and automatic enforcement procedures put in place by the Budget Control Act (BCA). After the first 10 years, this fiscal constraint is maintained; revenue and spending other than interest on the debt and large entitlement programs (Social Security, Medicare, and Medicaid) are held constant as a share of gross domestic product (GDP). Over the long term, revenue as a share of GDP is higher and discretionary spending lower than historical averages.

In the Alternative simulation, expiring tax provisions are extended to 2022, and the alternative minimum tax (AMT) exemption amount is indexed to inflation through 2022; revenues are then brought back to the historical average as a share of GDP. For the first 10 years, discretionary spending reflects the original caps set by the BCA but not the lower caps triggered by the automatic enforcement procedures. Over the long term, discretionary spending and revenue are held at historical averages.

The Baseline Extended simulation follows the Trustees' 2011 intermediate projections for Social Security and Medicare and CBO's June 2011 long-term projections for Medicaid adjusted to reflect excess cost growth consistent with the Trustees' Medicare projections.

In the Alternative simulation, Medicare spending is based on the Centers for Medicare & Medicaid Services Office of the Actuary's (CMS Actuary) alternative projections that assume reductions in Medicare physician rates do not occur as scheduled under current law and that certain cost-containment mechanisms intended to slow the growth of health care cost are not sustained over the long term. GAO also shows the outlook using CBO's long-term projections for Social Security and the major health entitlements; the 2022 and the 2022. For the first 10 years, discretionary spending reflects the original caps set by the BCA but not the lower caps triggered by the automatic enforcement procedures. Over the long term, discretionary spending and revenue are held at historical averages.

The Baseline Extended simulation follows the Trustees' 2011 intermediate projections for Social Security and Medicare and CBO's June 2011 long-term projections for Medicaid adjusted to reflect excess cost growth consistent with the Trustees' projections. In the Alternative simulation, Medicare spending is based on the Centers for Medicare & Medicaid Services Office of the Actuary's (CMS Actuary) alternative projections that assume reductions in Medicare physician rates do not occur as scheduled under current law and that certain cost- containment mechanisms intended to slow the growth of health care cost are not sustained over the long term. GAO also shows the outlook using CBO's long-term projections for Social Security and the major health entitlements; the results are consistent with GAO's simulations based largely on the Trustees.

Federal deficits and debt have reached historic highs in recent years. Congress has taken action to address the fiscal imbalance, but longer-term challenges remain. The Budget Control Act (BCA) of 2011 limits spending over the next decade and leads to an improved fiscal outlook. The act targets discretionary spending, and under both of GAO's simulations, discretionary spending as a share of the economy would be lower in 2022 than at any point in the last 50 years. Further, as the economy recovers, revenue increases and spending decreases. While the BCA improved the outlook, it did not eliminate the longer-term challenge, in part because it did not focus on the fundamental drivers of the government's future fiscal imbalances—a structural gap between revenues and spending driven by rising health care costs and demographics. As our 2011 simulations showed, if the Patient Protection and Affordable Care Act (PPACA) is implemented as intended it would have a major effect on the gap but would not eliminate it. The aging of the population and rising health care costs will continue putting upward pressure on spending. Assuming revenue in the long term returns to the 40-year historical average and remains stable at that share of GDP, the imbalance between spending and revenues increases, resulting in increasing levels of debt held by the public.

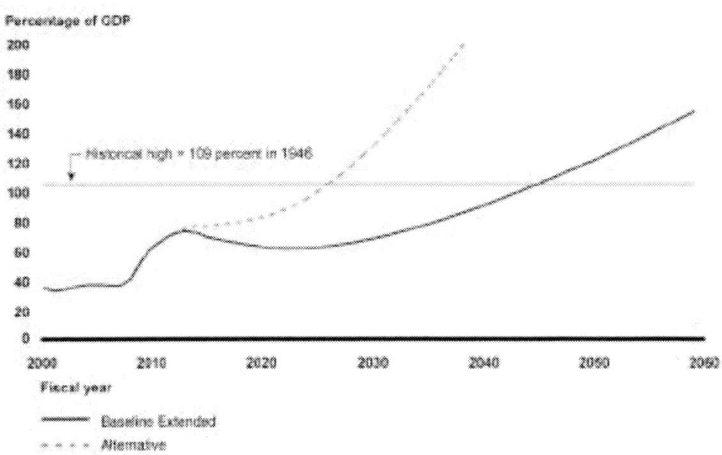

Source: GAO.

Note: Data are from GAO's Spring 2012 simulations based on the Trustees' assumptions for Social Security and the Trustees' and the CMS Actuary's assumptions for Medicare.

Figure 1. Debt Held by the Public under Two Fiscal Policy Simulations.

A continuing increase in debt as a share of GDP means the federal government is on an unsustainable long-term fiscal path and underscores the need for policymakers to act to change the path. See figure 1.

The pace at which deficits grow and the resulting debt buildup vary depending on the assumptions used: deficits and debt grow less rapidly in the Baseline Extended simulation than under the Alternative simulation, which has both lower revenues and higher spending levels than the Baseline Extended simulation. Under the Baseline Extended simulation, debt held by the public would exceed its post–World War II historical high of 109 percent of GDP by 2048; under the Alternative simulation it would cross this threshold by 2026.

The growing fiscal imbalance is driven on the spending side by rising health care costs and the aging of the population. The oldest members of the baby-boom generation are already eligible for Social Security retirement benefits and for Medicare. The Social Security program, which historically ran large cash surpluses that helped reduce the need to borrow from the public to finance other programs, is now projected to pay more in benefits than it receives in tax income each year into the future.[1] Although health care spending growth recently slowed, it has been growing faster than the overall economy and is expected to continue to grow at an increased rate as more members of the baby-boom generation become eligible for federal health programs.

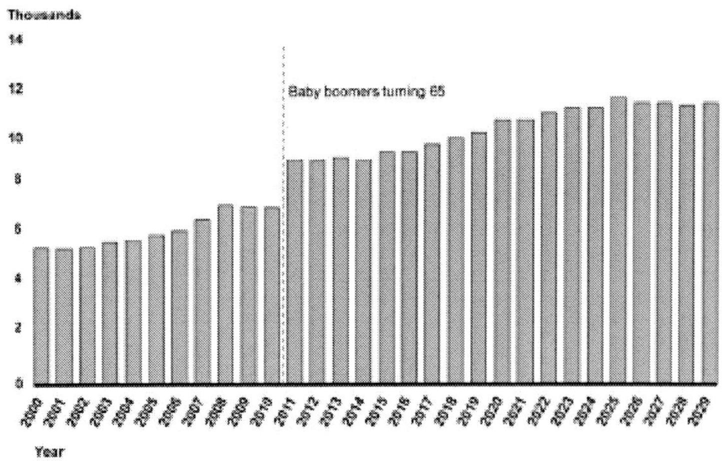

Source: GAO analysis of US Census Bureau data.

Note: Data are from the U.S. Census Bureau's National Population Projections. For this analysis, we used data from the low net international migration series.

Figure 2. Daily Average Number of People Turning 65 Each Year.

As shown in figure 2, the number of baby boomers turning 65 is projected to grow in coming years, averaging about 7,600 per day in 2011, and about 11,400 per day by 2029.

Several provisions of PPACA were designed to control the growth of health care costs. The full implementation and effectiveness of these cost-control provisions, which are reflected in the Baseline Extended simulation, would slow the growth in federal health care spending over the long term. Under the Baseline Extended simulation, spending on Medicare and Medicaid grows from 5 percent of GDP in 2010 to over 7 percent by 2030.There are, however, significant uncertainties surrounding the growth of health care costs. Spending is influenced not only by policies and laws, but also by future demographic and economic trends, development and deployment of medical technology, the cost and availability of insurance, and the responses of health care providers, consumers, and policymakers to these trends. The Trustees, CBO, and the CMS Actuary have expressed concerns about the sustainability of certain health care cost-control measures over the long term. For example, they note that reductions in physician payment rates scheduled to occur under current law have routinely been overridden.

They have also questioned whether a provision in PPACA that would restrain spending growth by reducing the payment rates for certain Medicare services based on productivity gains observed throughout the economy is sustainable over the long term. According to CMS, health care productivity gains have historically been small, and may be difficult to achieve in the future due to several factors, including the labor-intensive nature of the industry and the individual customization of treatments in many cases. These concerns are reflected in our Alternative simulation, which, consistent with CBO's and the CMS Actuary's alternative scenarios, assumes that certain cost-containment mechanisms are not sustained over the long term.[2] Spending on health care grows much more rapidly under this more pessimistic set of assumptions. Absent changes to these programs, spending on Medicare and Medicaid under the Alternative simulation grows to over 8 percent of GDP by 2030.

Under either set of assumptions about health care cost growth, spending for the major health and retirement programs will increase, putting greater pressure on the rest of the federal budget. In 2010, about 47 cents of every federal dollar spent went to Social Security, Medicare, Medicaid, and interest on the federal debt. Figures 3 and 4 below show revenue and the composition of spending under the Baseline Extended and Alternative simulations moving forward.

Under the Baseline Extended simulation, revenues as a share of the economy are higher and discretionary spending is lower than historical averages.

As figure 3 shows, spending on Social Security, Medicare, Medicaid, and interest would grow to about 70 cents of every dollar spent by 2040. By this time, there is little room for "all other spending," which includes not only national defense, homeland security, veteran's health care, and investment in highways and mass transit, but also smaller entitlement programs such as farm price supports and student loans.

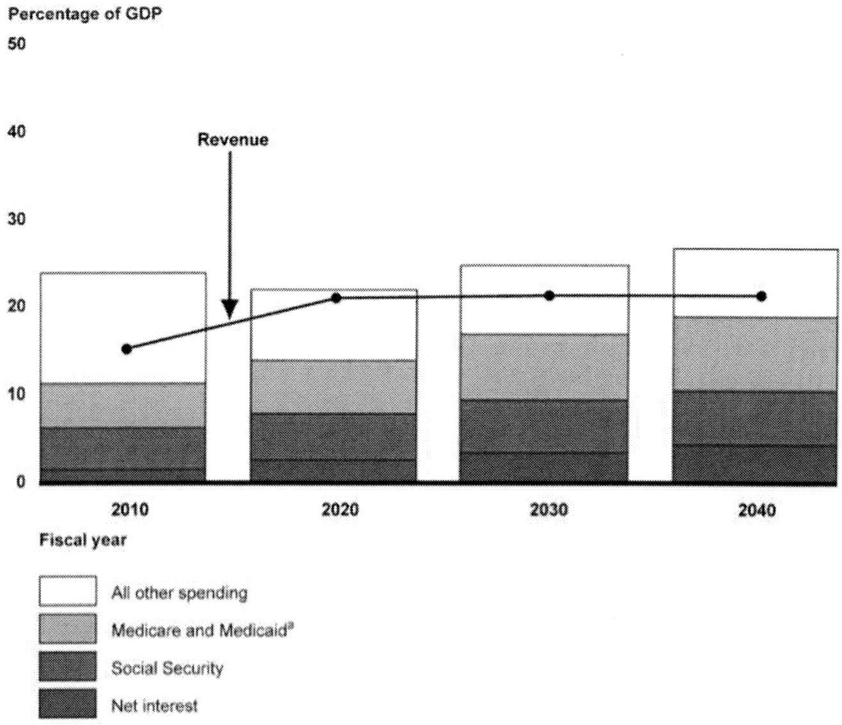

Source: GAO.

Notes: Data are from GAO's Spring 2012 simulations based on the Trustees' assumptions for Social Security and the Trustees' and the CMS Actuary's assumptions for Medicare.

[a]This also includes spending for insurance exchange subsidies and the Children's Health Insurance Program.

Figure 3. Potential Fiscal Outcomes under the Baseline Extended Simulation: Revenues and Composition of Spending.

In the Alternative simulation, revenue and discretionary spending are at their historical averages over the long term. In this simulation, spending on Social Security, Medicare, Medicaid, and interest exceeds revenues by 2030 and by 2040, 73 cents of every federal dollar spent would go to these categories.

Overall, our simulations illustrate the difficult trade-offs that policymakers will have to consider in order to rebalance the federal government's fiscal position.

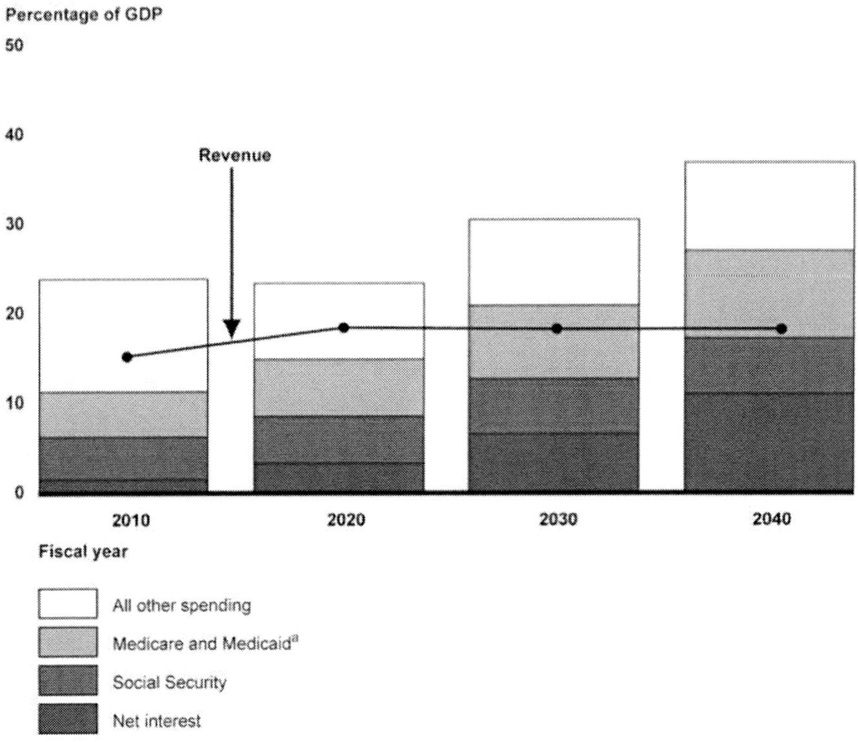

Source: GAO.

Notes: Data are from GAO's Spring 2012 simulations based on the Trustees' assumptions for Social Security and the Trustees' and the CMS Actuary's assumptions for Medicare.

[a]This also includes spending for insurance exchange subsidies and the Children's Health Insurance Program.

Figure 4. Potential Fiscal Outcomes under the Alternative Simulation: Revenues and Composition of Spending.

BALANCING NEAR-TERM AND LONG-TERM CONSIDERATIONS

When considering action to address the longer-term fiscal challenge, it is important to balance the near-term effects. One tool used to measure the challenge over the long term is the "fiscal gap." The fiscal gap represents the difference, or gap, between revenue and noninterest spending in present value terms over a certain period, such as 75 years, that would need to be closed in order to achieve a specified debt level (e.g., today's debt to GDP ratio) at the end of the period. From the fiscal gap, one can calculate the size of action needed—in terms of tax increases, spending reductions, or, more likely, some combination of the two—to close the gap.

For example, under our Alternative simulation, the fiscal gap is 8.2 percent of GDP (see table 1). This means that, on average over the next 75 years, revenue would have to increase by more than 45 percent or noninterest spending would have to be reduced by about 32 percent (or some combination of the two) to keep debt held by the public at the end of the period from exceeding its level at the beginning of 2012 (roughly 68 percent of GDP). Even-more significant changes would be needed to reduce debt to lower levels.

Table 1. Federal Fiscal Gap under GAO's Simulations

		Average percentage change required to close gap			
		If action is taken today		If action is delayed until 2022	
Simulation	Fiscal gap 2012–2086 (percent of GDP)	Solely through increases in revenue	Solely through decreases in noninterest spending	Solely through increases in revenue	Solely through decreases in noninterest spending
Baseline Extended	1.8	8.4	8.0	9.9	9.4
Alternative	8.2	45.7	32.2	54.3	37.0

Source: GAO.

Note: Data are from GAO's Spring 2012 simulations based on the Trustees' assumptions for Social Security and the Trustees' and CMS Actuary's assumptions for Medicare.

While immediate action would reduce the size of the changes necessary to close the fiscal gap, the risk to near-term economic growth is also a factor. With this in mind, policy changes could be designed to phase in over time allowing for the economy to fully recover and for people to adjust to the changes.

Table 1 illustrates how much greater fiscal policy changes would have to be if no actions were taken for the next decade. Such a delay would increase the risk that the eventual changes will be disruptive and destabilizing. Under our Alternative simulation, waiting 10 years would increase the fiscal gap to nearly 10 percent of GDP— meaning a revenue increase of about 54 percent or a noninterest spending cut of 37 percent or some combination of the two would be required to bring debt held by the public back to today's level by 2086.

CONCLUDING OBSERVATIONS

The economy continues to recover from the nation's most severe recession since the end of World War II, and while there are calls for continued federal action to support the economy, these must be balanced with the need to act soon to develop a plan for addressing the long-term fiscal imbalance. Absent policy changes, increasingly significant changes will be needed to close the fiscal gap. However, action taken to address the fiscal outlook needs to be balanced with the importance of sustaining economic growth in the near term. If policy changes designed to correct the federal government's fiscal path are too sharp, they could stifle the pace of the recovery in the near term. Conversely, changes in policy designed to encourage near-term recovery could worsen the long-term outlook and increase the size of necessary changes in the long run.

Our simulations show deficits declining over the next several years, but this trend reverses before the decade is over under the assumptions in our simulations.

Despite limits on discretionary spending that would bring discretionary spending to levels not seen in recent history, our simulations show total federal spending continuing to exceed revenues and feeding an unsustainable growth in debt.

The policy actions required to close the fiscal gap are significant, and changing the long-term outlook will likely require difficult decisions about both federal spending and revenue.

CHANGES SINCE THE LAST UPDATE

This update incorporates CBO's January 2012 baseline projections that follow current law at that time.[3] A key change from CBO's prior baseline estimates—and our prior long-term fiscal outlook update—was the treatment of deficit reduction related to the BCA. At the time of our last update in fall 2011, it was not known whether lawmakers would enact legislation originating from the Joint Select Committee on Deficit Reduction, and thus whether such legislation or the Budget Control Act's automatic enforcement procedures would be implemented. Therefore, we assumed that deficit reduction resulting from the act would take effect under both the Baseline Extended and the Alternative simulations, but did not make assumptions about the allocation between spending and revenues. Because no such legislation was enacted, CBO's January 2012 baseline reflects the act's automatic procedures—cuts among discretionary, Medicare, and other mandatory spending—that go into effect under current law. Consistent with CBO's baseline, our Baseline Extended simulation also reflects the changes to discretionary and mandatory spending under the automatic enforcement procedures. However, we do not apply the effects of the automatic enforcement procedures to the Alternative simulation in this update. In this regard, our Alternative simulation is consistent with the alternative scenario CBO described in its January 2012 update.

KEY ASSUMPTIONS IN OUR FEDERAL SIMULATIONS

Table 2 lists the key assumptions incorporated in the Baseline Extended and Alternative simulations based on the Trustees' assumptions for Social Security and the Trustees' and CMS Actuary's assumptions for Medicare.

Table 3 shows the key economic assumptions that underlie all of our simulations.

GDP is held constant across simulations and does not respond to changes in fiscal policy. Also, the implied interest rate on federal debt held by the public in our simulations is held constant over the long term even when deficits climb.

With large budget deficits, there could be a rise in the rate of interest and a more rapid increase in federal interest payments than our simulations display.

Table 2. Assumptions for Baseline Extended and Alternative Simulations

Model inputs	Baseline Extended simulation	Alternative simulation
Revenue	CBO's January 2012 baseline that assumes tax cutswill expire as scheduled under current law and that an increasing share of taxpayers will be subject to higher tax rates through 2022; thereafter remains constant at 21.0 percent of GDP (CBO's projection in 2022)[a]	CBO's estimates assuming expiring taxprovisions other than the temporary Social Security payroll tax reduction are extended through 2022, and the 2011 alternative minimum tax (AMT) exemption amount is indexed to inflation for years 2012–2022; thereafter is phased into the 40-year historical average of 17.9 percent of GDP
Social Security spending	CBO's January 2012 baseline through 2022; thereafter based on 2011 Social Security Trustees' intermediate projections	Same as Baseline Extended
Medicare spending	CBO's January 2012 baseline through 2022 that assumes cuts in physician payment rates will occur as scheduled under current law at the time[b] and that the implementation of the Budget Control Act's automatic enforcement procedures reduces spending;[c] thereafter 2011 Medicare Trustees' intermediate projections	Based on CMS Actuary's alternative scenario that assumes that physician payment rates grow with inflation (using the Medicare Economic Index)[d] in all future years, that spending reductions under the BCA do not occur, and policies that would restrain spending growth are applied fully through 2019 but begin to phase out thereafter
Medicaid, the Children's Health Insurance Program, and exchange subsidies spending	CBO's January 2012 baseline through 2022; thereafter CBO's June 2011 long-term projections adjusted to reflect excess cost growth consistent with the 2011 Medicare Trustees' intermediate projections	CBO's January 2012 baseline through 2022; thereafter CBO's 2011 long-term projections adjusted to reflect excess cost growth consistent with CMS Actuary's alternative scenario and CBO's alternative assumption that a policy that would slow the growth of subsidies for health insurance coverage is not in effect

Table 2. (Continued)

Model inputs	Baseline Extended simulation	Alternative simulation
Other mandatory spending	CBO's January 2012 baseline through 2022, which incorporates the reductions in spending scheduled to occur under the Budget Control Act's automatic enforcement procedures; thereafter remains constant as a share of GDP at 2.3 percent of GDP (implied by CBO's projection in 2022)	Baseline Extended adjusted for extension of certain tax credits and to exclude the effects of the Budget Control Act's automatic enforcement procedures through 2022; thereafter is phased back to 2.3 percent of GDP by 2025 (same as Baseline Extended)
Discretionary spending	CBO's January 2012 baseline through 2022, which reflects the original caps set by the Budget Control Act, as well as the lower caps triggered by the automatic enforcement procedures; thereafter remains constant at 5.6 percent of GDP (CBO's projection in 2022)	Follows the original caps set by the Budget Control Act but not the lower caps triggered by the act's automatic enforcement procedures; after 2022 it gradually phases to 7.5 percent of GDP (the 20-year historical average)

Source: GAO.

Notes: CBO's projections are from The Budget and Economic Outlook: Fiscal Years 2012 to 2022 (January 2012) and CBO's 2011 Long-Term Budget Outlook (June 2011). Trustees projections are from The 2011 Annual Report of the Board of Trustees of the Federal Old-Age and Survivors Insurance and Federal Disability Insurance Trust Funds and The 2011 Annual Report of the Boards of Trustees of the Federal Hospital Insurance and Federal Supplementary Medical Insurance Trust Funds, which were both issued on May 13, 2011. Projections from the CMS Actuary are based on Projected Medicare Expenditures under an Illustrative Scenario with Alternative Payment Updates to Medicare Providers (May 13, 2011). We assume that Social Security and Medicare benefits are paid in full regardless of the amounts available in the trust funds.

[a] Both simulations assume that the temporary Social Security payroll tax reduction would expire at the end of February 2012. However, the Middle Class Tax Relief and Job Creation Act of 2012 (Pub. L. No. 112-96) extended the reduction through the end of December 2012. The act did not offset the cost of the extended reduction, but we expect that the change would have a minimal effect on the overall outlook.

[b] The Middle Class Tax Relief and Job Creation Act prevented scheduled cuts in reimbursement rates to physicians for 2012 that were assumed to occur under CBO's January 2012 baseline projections. We did not incorporate the effects of this override into the Baseline Extended simulation. Because the act included

provisions to offset the costs of the extension, it would have a minimal effect on the longer-term fiscal outlook.

[c] The Budget Control Act established limits on discretionary budget authority for 2013 through 2021. In addition, it specified additional limits on discretionary spending and automatic reductions in mandatory spending, including Medicare, that would take effect if lawmakers did not enact legislation originating from the Joint Select Committee on Deficit Reduction that would reduce projected deficits by at least $1.2 trillion. Because no such legislation was enacted, those procedures are now scheduled to go into effect.

[d] Since 2003, Congress took a series of legislative actions to prevent scheduled reductions in physician payment rates that would otherwise occur under law. Physician fee updates set by Congress have averaged 0.9 percent per year over this period. Growth in the Medicare Economic Index is projected to average 1.9 percent from 2012 to 2020. Thus, the assumption used by CMS, and in our Alternative simulation, implies physician payment rates will grow almost two times faster than they have since 2003.

Table 3. Key Economic Assumptions Underlying All of GAO's Long-Term Federal Simulations

Model inputs	All simulations
Real GDP Growth	CBO's January 2012 baseline through 2022; thereafter averages 2.1 percent based on the intermediate assumptions of the 2011 Social Security and Medicare Trustees reports
Inflation (percentage change in GDP price index)	CBO's January 2012 baseline through 2022; 2.0 percent thereafter (CBO's projection in 2022)
Interest rate (on publicly held debt)	Rate implied by CBO's January 2012 baseline net interest payment projections through 2022; phasing to5.2 percent in 2025 and then constant thereafter (CBO's June 2011 long-term projection)

Source: GAO.

A more detailed description of the federal model and key assumptions can be found at www.gao.gov/special.pubs/longterm/fed/aboutlongterm.html.

The simulation results depend largely on what is assumed about growth in large entitlement programs. As in previous updates, we also show the Baseline Extended simulation using CBO estimates for long-term spending on Social Security and major health entitlement programs (Medicare, Medicaid, and others). In addition, we show the Alternative simulation using different assumptions about certain health care cost-containment provisions based on

CBO alternative projections. As figure 5 shows, the results are similar to our simulations using the Trustees and CMS Actuary's projections.

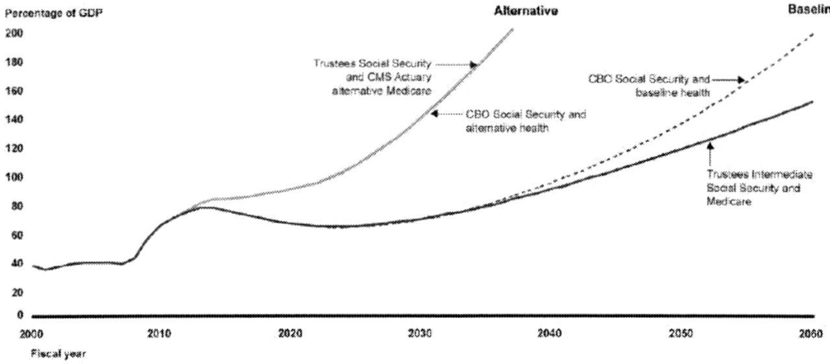

Source: GAO.

Note: The two Alternative simulations are so close that their separate lines are not visible on this graph.

Table 4 shows the CBO assumptions incorporated into the simulations that were used in the comparison shown in figure 5.

This product is part of a body of work on federal debt and the long-term fiscal challenge. Related products can be found at www.gao.gov/special.pubs/longterm/past/. We conducted our work from January 2012 to April 2012 in accordance with all sections of GAO's Quality Assurance Framework that are relevant to our objectives. The framework requires that we plan and perform the engagement to obtain sufficient and appropriate evidence to meet our stated objectives and to discuss any limitations in our work. We believe that the information and data obtained, and the analysis conducted, provide a reasonable basis for any findings and conclusions in this product.

Table 4. Key Assumptions Underlying GAO's Simulations Using CBO's Spending Projections for Major Entitlement Programs

Model inputs	Baseline Extended simulation	Alternative simulation
Social Security spending	CBO's January 2012 baseline through 2022; thereafter based on CBO's June 2011 long-term projections for Social Security	Same as Baseline Extended
Medicare spending	CBO's January 2012 baseline through 2022; thereafter based	Based on CBO's projections under its alternative fiscal

Model inputs	Baseline Extended simulation	Alternative simulation
	on CBO's June 2011 long-term projections under its extended-baseline scenario	scenario that assume physician payment rates are maintained at 2011 levels through 2022 and that policies to restrain growth are not in effect after 2021
Medicaid, the Children's Health Insurance Program, and exchange subsidies spending	CBO's January 2012 baseline through 2022; thereafter based on CBO's June 2011 long-term projections under its extended-baseline scenario	CBO's January 2012 baseline through 2022; thereafter CBO's June 2011 projections under its alternative fiscal scenario in which a policy that would slow the growth of per-participant subsidies for health insurance coverage is assumed not to be in effect and eligibility thresholds are assumed to be modified to maintain the share of the population eligible for subsidies

Source: GAO.

Notes: CBO's projections are from CBO's 2011 Long-Term Budget Outlook (June 2011). CBO assumes that full benefits are paid regardless of the amounts available in the trust funds.

End Notes

[1] Social Security trust fund assets and reserves are used to make up the annual cash deficit. The Trustees project that trust fund reserves will be exhausted by 2036. See the Board of Trustees, Federal Old-Age and Survivors Insurance and Federal Disability Insurance Trust Funds, The 2011 Annual Report of the Board of Trustees of the Federal Old-Age and Survivors Insurance and Federal Disability Insurance Trust Funds (Washington, D.C.: May 13, 2011).

[2] While both CBO and the CMS Actuary assume that certain cost-containment mechanisms are not sustained, they make different assumptions that affect spending on health care. For example, CBO's assumes that physician payment rates are maintained at 2011 levels. In the CMS Actuary's alternative scenario, physician payment rates grow with inflation (using the Medicare Economic Index), which results in higher spending than under CBO's assumption.

[3] The CBO report is available at www.cbo.gov. When CBO analyzes the President's budget proposals, usually in March, it also updates its baseline. This year CBO's update includes the effects of the Middle Class Tax Relief and Job Creation Act of 2012 (Pub. L. No. 112-96) that was enacted on February 22, 2012 and extended the payroll tax reduction and

emergency unemployment insurance benefits through the end of December 2012 and prevented scheduled cuts in reimbursement rates to physicians. Consistent with past practice, we use the January baseline and so do not include the effects of that legislation. Doing so would have only minimal effect on the longer-term fiscal outlook.

INDEX

F

G

H

I

J

L

M

N

O

P

R

S

T

U

V

W

Y